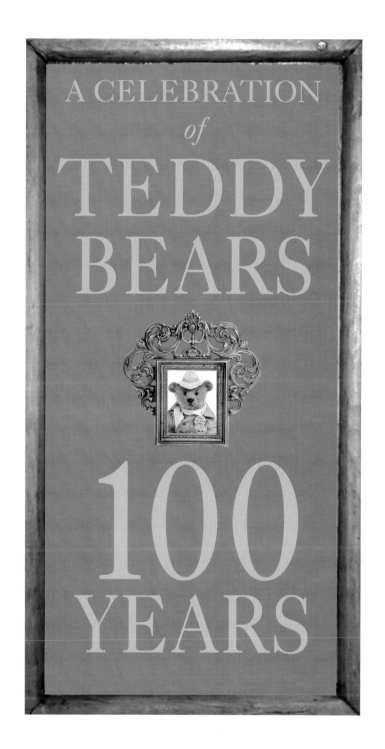

A CELEBRATION

of

TEDDY BEARS

100 YEARS

Acknowledgments:
A special thank you to Sue and Michael Pearson For their permission to use Teddy Bear images from their collection.

Published in 2002 by Caxton Editions
20 Bloomsbury Street
London WC1B 3JH
a member of the Caxton Publishing Group

Designed and produced for Caxton Editions
by Open Door Limited
Langham, Rutland
Editing: Mary Morton
Photography: Michael Pearson
Colour separation: GA Graphics, Stamford

Title: A Celebration of Teddy Bears
ISBN: 1 84067 394 X

A CELEBRATION

of

TEDDY BEARS 100 YEARS

CAXTON EDITIONS

CONTENTS

CONTENTS

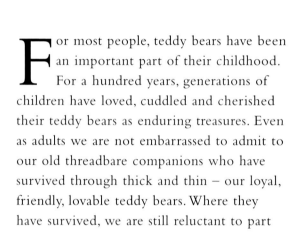

INTRODUCING THE TEDDY BEAR

Me and my Teddy Bear

Have no worries, have no cares.

Me and my Teddy Bear

Just play and play all day

For most people, teddy bears have been an important part of their childhood. For a hundred years, generations of children have loved, cuddled and cherished their teddy bears as enduring treasures. Even as adults we are not embarrassed to admit to our old threadbare companions who have survived through thick and thin – our loyal, friendly, lovable teddy bears. Where they have survived, we are still reluctant to part with them.

No two teddy bears are ever the same. Each has his or her own unique characteristics and this book traces the origins, history and makers of teddy bears from 1903 until the present day. The teddy bear in the 21st century is still the most popular mascot and talisman of childhood ever invented, the hero of countless stories, songs and poems. He (or she) shows no sign of disappearing from the magic world of play.

From the very beginning, the teddy bear has been made in all shapes, colours and sizes. Today, it still has a wide range of endearing expressions and is still capable of an extensive repertoire of actions.

Right: A classic humped-back Steiff bear.

The birth of the adorable teddy bear is surrounded by numerous stories and legends. It is generally agreed that America and Germany were simultaneously responsible for the origination, and the arrival of the teddy bear had an immediate impact which resulted in suppliers being unable to satisfy demand.

Over the years, the classic teddy bear has gradually evolved. And although various aspects of appearance have been experimented with, the basic appeal of the teddy bear remains as irresistible to children of all ages as it was a century ago.

Left: A well loved early Steiff bear.

A TEDDY BEAR LOVE AFFAIR

When I was only four days old

You came to live with me

And gave me all the love you hold

Quite unreservedly.

Oh Teddy Bear I still love thee

As much as I did then,

Though now we both are forty-three

And very nearly men.

"To My Teddy"
Anon

A love affair with a teddy bear is like no other love affair. If you fell in love with your first teddy bear, you will know that nothing was ever quite the same after that first heady surge of enchantment. And with each new teddy bear, it is love at first sight. No-one can ever quite explain why.

Once you really and truly fall in love with a teddy bear, whether you end up buying bears, making bears or collecting bears, you will probably find yourself unable to resist dressing them, repairing them, restoring them and giving up your home to them.

This book is all about teddy bears. In the past hundred years, they have rocketed from obscurity to super-stardom. It is about the

people who make teddy bears, and the people who fall in love with them – and end up sharing their lives with them.

With teddy bears, there is no such thing as monogamy or divorce. You can't collect husbands and wives – but with teddy bears you never have to choose between two passionate relationships – you can collect and love as many of them as you like. Somehow there is always room for just one more.

Bear fever began in 1902. It raged across the United States and Europe. Billions of bears have been made and sold since then. Two world wars, manufacturing and production shortages, trade bans and economic depressions have all failed to halt the

A TEDDY BEAR LOVE AFFAIR

amazing rise in the popularity of this bundle of cuddly fur, which comes in so many designs and in all colours and sizes. Demand continues to rise and production increases to satisfy the apparently insatiable appetite of consumers of all ages for teddy bears.

It is almost certain that for many people, their beloved teddy bear is the first gift they remember receiving that they have truly treasured. Some teddy bears have been loved so much that they have eventually just fallen to pieces. They really were loved to death. Others have survived – grubby, bald, patched and battle-scarred, but still

recognisable and still cherished. You will never, ever be able to forget that first teddy bear you loved so much. And if it is no longer with you, there will always be a place for it in your heart.

Classic bears, vintage bears, artist bears, home-made bears, dressed bears (undressed bears), replica bears, musical bears, mascot bears, bears with names and anonymous bears; bear pictures, stories, poems, songs and rhymes, bear memorabilia, bear museums, books and magazines, bear fairs and fan clubs – your love affair could be just beginning....

Left: The larger of the two bears is "Tubby" a beautiful Steiff bear dating from 1910; see page 39 for Tubby's story.

Overleaf: A 1907 Steiff.

THE TEDDY BEAR STORY

A bear, however hard he tries,

Grows tubby without exercise.

Our teddy bear is short and fat,

Which is not to be wondered at.

But do you think it worries him

To know that he is far from slim?

No, just the other way about –

He's proud of being short and stout.

Teddy Bear
A. A. Milne

Teddy bear history includes stories about the earliest designers and manufacturers. It crosses continents, ignores social, political, economic and cultural barriers and touches the heart of everyone who has ever owned and loved a teddy bear. The history of teddy bears is no respecter of age.

The real story of the teddy bear started in the middle of the 19th century. It is a remarkable story. And this is how it all began.

The Little Crippled Girl
The Story of Margarete Steiff

Once upon a time, which is the best beginning for all stories, there was a little girl who couldn't walk. Her name was Margarete Steiff and she was born in a small village

called Giengen an der Brenz in Germany, in 1847. While Margarete was still very young she caught polio. The rest of her childhood was spent paralysed, and in a wheelchair. Although Margarete was blessed with great spirit and optimism, she could only dream of running, jumping and climbing whilst she watched her brothers play the games she would have loved to join in.

There were very few opportunities for a teenager like Margarete to train to earn a living in Germany in the 1860s. To begin with, she was a girl and, in those days, girls were expected to marry and have babies. Some girls did work, but her disability restricted even the few choices which she might have had. Of limited mobility, living in an obscure European town and totally dependent on her family's limited resources, it was hard to know how this crippled girl could occupy herself. Clearly her chances of

marriage would be slim. She was unable to do housework or even care for herself. And yet highly intelligent, with a bright enquiring mind, Margarete Steiff hated to be idle.

Although she realised it would be a terrible struggle, she decided to study needlework and eventually mastered the intricacies of a sewing machine. It was hard and there were many setbacks for Margarete Steiff. Almost everything about her background and circumstances was against her. But in spite of the most daunting odds, by the time she was 30 years old, she was successfully making and selling ladies' and children's clothes from her own shop. One Christmas she decided to make a few elephant pin cushions for some of her customers. They were very popular.

From Rags to Riches

In spite of her disabilities, Margarete's business grew quickly and became profitable. She was imaginative, determined and had a great sense of fun. Although she never married, she loved children. Her elephant pin cushions were so successful that she experimented with other patterns and she made stuffed toys for her nephews and nieces using odd pieces of felt left over from her uncle's fabric factory. The children adored the special presents made for them by their aunt.

These gifts were so successful that Margarete began to experiment. She tried out all sorts of animals – dogs, monkeys, camels and donkeys. They were beautifully made, with great attention to detail. Her family and friends were enchanted. Fritz, her brother, decided that he would try and sell her

unusual toys in local markets. They were a wild success. Margarete formed a mail order company for her soft toys and soon found it hard to keep up with demand, so she employed workers to help her.

In 1893, when Margarete was 46, Steiff became a registered company. By the turn of the century, her toy-making business was so successful that five of her nephews had joined her. It was Richard Steiff, one of the nephews, who became the creative force for the next generation.

Young Richard had been an art student in Stuttgart. He had spent many hours watching the bears perform at the Nill zoo between his art classes. He was fascinated by bears and made many drawings and sketches in his spare time. The performing bears he watched so often must have inspired him to create his very own toy bear. At first, the bears he designed and made were rigid and could only stand upright or on all fours like the real bears he loved so much. He worked closely with his aunt and his rigid bears featured in the Steiff catalogues for ten years. Then, one day, Richard had a brainwave. What if he could make a toy bear that was soft and cuddly that children could really play with? He looked carefully at the dolls that were being made for little girls. They had appealing faces; their heads, arms and legs were jointed and could move realistically. He decided to try and make a fully jointed bear of his very own. Using a rich golden-coloured plush fur material, Richard's teddy bear – though it was not called that at the time – could actually move its head, arms and legs. It had a lovely face with little black boot-button eyes and a black stitched

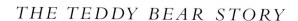

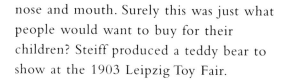

nose and mouth. Surely this was just what people would want to buy for their children? Steiff produced a teddy bear to show at the 1903 Leipzig Toy Fair.

At first, Richard was disappointed. The new bear was not a great success at the fair, and Richard was about to pack up and go home when an American buyer for a large toy firm passed his stand. He saw the bear – and instantly fell in love with it immediately. He ordered 3,000 of Richard Steiff's bears and had them shipped to the United States. A legend was about to be created. Teddy bear fever had begun. The rest of the story for the Steiffs reads like a fairy tale come true.

Between 1903 and 1905, Margarete and Richard, who shared extremely high standards, worked together to improve and perfect this first jointed bear. The design was altered and refined again and again; production methods were streamlined. The teddy bear we know and love today had been born.

1907 became known as "The Year of the Bear". An amazing one million teddy bears were sold and Margarete, a perfectionist, was at last satisfied with Richard's work. The Steiff trademark of a "Button in the Ear" was patented to try and stop other teddy bear manufacturers from copying their popular designs.

Right: Two Steiff bears dating from 1907 and 1908, both with the typical long shaved muzzles and cupped ears found on early Steiff bears.

Perhaps because he was an innovator at heart, or maybe because he loved the animals so much, Richard Steiff never stopped experimenting with his designs and was continually reinventing his original teddy bear. Steiff bears, with their delightful little faces, appeared in many sizes and colours, always with amazing attention to detail, and care was taken to satisfy the demands of different markets, always giving the customers the bears which most appealed to them.

By the time she died in 1909, aged 62, Margarete Steiff, the little crippled girl who had sat and watched other children play, had inspired an industry which was to give millions of children throughout the world their first very own love affair.

After Margarete's death, her brothers and nephews carried on the Steiff family business, and the company continued to prosper. But in 1914, with the onset of the First World War, Richard, Paul and Hugo Steiff were called up to fight for their country. The exports of teddy bears dried up because Germany was at war and no-one abroad wanted German-made products any more. Output from the Steiff factory was also reduced drastically because the German government insisted that the premises be used for the production of war munitions. The German war effort did not include making teddy bears.

THE TEDDY BEAR STORY

After the end of the war, things gradually returned to normal in Germany. Steiff began to produce a range of teddy bears again. Because materials were in short supply, paper plush was used instead of mohair. Manufacturing methods were modernised using a conveyor-belt system, and costs were reduced so that teddy bears could be bought by the mass market. Sales and output grew.

Many new designs appeared in the years between the wars. More colourful, softer and lighter bears sold extremely well. With the addition of a range of novelty bears, the Steiff business expanded once more and the inter-war years were prosperous. By 1939, 20 years after her death, Margarete Steiff was destined never to be forgotten. Today, one hundred years after the appearance of the first real teddy bear, the name of Steiff means only one thing. Teddy bears.

Left: This 1904 rod bear is very rare. He has metal rods connecting his joints, very long arms and black button eyes.

HOW TEDDY GOT HIS NAME

If you go down to the woods today

You'd better not go alone

It's lovely down in the woods today

But safer to stay at home

From The Teddy bears Picnic
Jimmy kennedy 1902–1984

How did the ferocious bear become our adored teddy bear? Back in the 19th century, dancing bears, performing in the streets, were a familiar sight. They always drew crowds of people. Transported from town to town across Europe, the enormous captive bears, with their mix of dangerous and cuddly, provided a great thrill for adults and children alike. Dancing bears were first-rate entertainment for the whole family.

By the turn of the century, postcards with realistic pictures of grizzly bears were popular everywhere. Perhaps it was the cruel sport of bear-baiting which inspired many of the early drawings and ornaments, depicting bears bound in chains or with rings through their noses.

Right: A Steiff Record Teddy mounted on a metal chassis and wooden wheels.

In Germany and Switzerland, the Black Forest wood carvers, using designs based on the performing bears, produced wonderfully realistic wooden replicas. People loved them, bought them for their homes and treasured them.

One of the most famous traditional folk tales of all time is *Goldilocks and the Three Bears*. Throughout the 19th century this story which was translated into many languages, beautifully illustrated and widely published to entertain generations of children.

It was only at the beginning of the 20th century that the first soft toys made their appearance. Standing on all fours, they were mounted on wheels, produced in France by Martin and Pintel and in Germany by the famous Steiff company.

16

HOW TEDDY GOT HIS NAME

Teddy's Bear

Of course there are several claims for producing the very first teddy bear. One of the most famous, and best documented, accounts comes from America.

Whilst the Steiff family were creating their bears in Germany, across the Atlantic an incident happened which inspired Clifford Berryman to draw a cartoon which became famous in bear history. This, undoubtedly, was what gave the first teddy bear its name.

In November 1902 the US president Theodore "Teddy" Roosevelt had been on a hunting trip in Mississippi. Because he failed to make a kill, his hosts caught a bear cub. They tied it to a tree and tried to persuade the president to shoot it as a sitting target. He refused with the immortal words;

"Spare the bear. I will never shoot a tethered animal."

On 16 November 1902, the story was reported in the *Washington Post* and it was illustrated by cartoonist Clifford Berryman who drew the act of mercy under the caption "Drawing the Line in Mississippi". The story of their soft-hearted president caught the imagination of the American public immediately.

Morris Mishcom was a recent Russian immigrant who owned a shop in Brooklyn, New York. His wife Rose, who had seen the Berryman cartoon, was amused and captivated by it. She decided to make a toy bear for her husband to display in his shop window just before Christmas with a copy of the cartoon. After requesting permission from the president himself, whose nickname was Teddy, the bear was named Teddy's Bear.

Overnight, America went bear mad and President Roosevelt found himself with a political mascot. The Mishcoms were suddenly in the toy-making business.

Left: This 1904 bear has googly eyes very much like the bear in the original Berryman cartoon. He is very rare with his original collar and ribbon.

HOW TEDDY GOT HIS NAME

The wholesale firm of Butler Brothers, who had seen Teddy's Bear and decided it was likely to be a commercial success, quickly bought up Mishcom's entire stock, and the money they paid him enabled Mishcom to set up his own business. Rose and Morris Mishcom established the Ideal Novelty & Toy Company which began to make teddy bears for the mass market. In America, teddy bear fever was raging and their company was an instant success.

By 1907, Morris Mishcom's teddy bear business was booming. He had headquarters in Newark, New Jersey, and had moved to much larger premises in Brownsville, Brooklyn. Rose and Morris's teddy bear designs, which were quite similar to the Steiff bears, changed very little until the beginning of the Second World War. But when Morris died in 1938 Benjamin Mishcom, his son, took over the family business. He introduced a range of new designs and materials and altered the name of the company to the Ideal Toy Corporation.

Right: A googly-eyed Ideal bear from 1905.

HOW TEDDY GOT HIS NAME

The early Ideal teddy bears had long snouts, large tapered feet and elongated arms with curved paws. The Americans loved them and bought them in huge quantities.

Some extraordinary novelty bears were made by the Columbia Teddy Bear Company in the early years and these were also very popular, especially the Laughing Roosevelt Bear, which opened its mouth to display large teeth just like those of the President. This bear was made in 1907. Ten years later the red, white and blue Patriotic Bear appeared with its electric light-bulb eyes. Today they fetch very high prices and are highly collectible.

One of the original googly-eyed Ideal bears was said to have been thrown from the back of a train by President Theodore Roosevelt during his 1904 election campaign. There is no report of whether the bear perished or whether some kind soul rescued him.

Following President Roosevelt's re-election, teddy bear fever in America reached its peak. A great many manufacturers began to make teddy bears which included both traditional designs and novelties.

In about 1907–1910, two Ideal soldier bears were made wearing Teddy Roosevelt Rough Rider outfits. Later they were given shoes and medals to wear. Both the bears are stuffed with excelsior and one has boot-button eyes whilst the eyes of his friend are made of glass. Perhaps they have survived well because only the visible parts of their bodies are made of mohair. The rest is made of cotton – and the design is similar to the dressed Bingie bears later made by Merrythought.

Teddy bears were loved so passionately by thousands of Americans that the early years of the 20th century became known as "the teddy bear years". Although production was dominated by Morris Mishcom's business, other important manufacturers quickly entered the market making all sorts of different bears from about 1910 onwards.

Left: An early American Ideal bear from 1905, complete with his original Rough Rider outfit.

Left: Teddy Loring, 1910, wearing a 1904 election campaign pin. This bear was given to John Alden Loring as a gift from Theodore Roosevelt in 1910.

19

HOW TEDDY GOT HIS NAME

Right: This laughing bear, 1908, opens his mouth when his tummy is squeezed to reveal two white glass teeth.

Many of the traditional teddy bears of that time closely resemble the German Steiffs and often have a realistic hump back and distinctively long arms. The Laughing Roosevelt Bear was made in a variety of designs. One of the earliest examples dates from 1907 and is known as a Laughing Burlap bear because he is made of an unusual brown nettle cloth material. He looks extremely fierce with his black boot-button eyes and very fierce-looking teeth and jaws. His long jointed body has very short arms. Another version, made a year later, was given short golden mohair fur, jointed arms and legs, a swivel head and glass eyes. When his tummy was squeezed his mouth opened revealing two white glass teeth set in his wooden jaw.

HOW TEDDY GOT HIS NAME

Left: Two
Knickerbocker
Toy company
bears.

Traditional, classic designs of excellent-quality novelty bears, including the Laughing Roosevelt Bear, and huge quantities of mass-produced teddy bears, flooded the toy shops. Companies such as The Character Toy Company, Aetna, Bruin, Gund and Knickerbocker all fed the demand for teddy bears. The Knickerbocker Toy Company was founded in Albany, New York, in 1869. Its business was the production of educational toys for children of all ages. The name was taken from the

first Dutch settlers who had been nicknamed "Knickerbocker" – because they always wore distinctive baggy knickerbocker trousers. It was not until 1920 that Knickerbocker began to make its first teddy bears and the company continued in business until the 1980s.

Today, like Steiff, many of these businesses are still making their own ranges of wonderful bears.

BEARS GO TO BRITAIN

The king just laughed as the train pulled out,

But he said to himself as he turned about,

'It would help me carry my country's cares,

If every home had teddy bears.'

Seymour Eaton

In January 1901, Britain had a new king. Edward VII came to the throne on the death of his mother Queen Victoria. A new age had begun and the king was nicknamed "Teddy". Within a year of his accession it was rumoured that the king had fallen in love. Although Edward the VII was a married man with a family, and was in his sixties, his reputation as a ladies' man was widely known. Society gossip about the king's latest love affair could not be kept secret. It was reported that he had been introduced to an Australian koala bear – and it was love at first sight. The king adored the unusual little bear. Teddy bear fever had reached the gracious nurseries of Edwardian Britain.

Right: A 1950's Dean's 'True to Life' bear.

Left: A typical
1912 Farnell
bear with a long
muzzle and
black stitched
nose.

The First British Bear

J. K. Farnell

The first real teddy bear in Britain is believed to have been made by J. K. Farnell in 1908. They probably used rabbit skins for their earliest toys, as well as using more conventional fabrics. It has been suggested that Farnell actually made a teddy bear several years before Steiff, but so far this has not been proved.

J. K. Farnell was founded in about 1840 in Notting Hill, London, by John Kirby Farnell. At first the business specialised in making pin cushions, tea cosies and decorative pen wipers – all vital household accessories with a substantial demand.

When John Farnell died in 1897, his son and daughter, Henry and Agnes, moved the family business from Notting Hill to Acton where they established a small toy factory in the garden of their 18th-century home.

Right: Two Farnell bears 1912 (left) and 1920 (right). Christopher Robin's bear, who became that superstar bear Winnie the Pooh, was an Alpha Farnell bear.

From the beginning, Agnes Farnell was closely involved with the design and production of the delightful Farnell bears, which had distinctive slightly upturned noses, and were in great demand for little British children even before the outbreak of the First World War in 1914.

Like the early Steiff bears, the first teddy bears from the Farnell factory had a definite hump back and distinctive shiny black button eyes. The long silky golden mohair fur was one of the most attractive characteristics of Farnell's bears, and each one always had a long shaved muzzle.

Harrods' London shop sold huge quantities of Farnell bears from 1915 onwards, and the teddy bear which was bought for little Christopher Robin Milne as a first birthday present became the world-famous Winnie the Pooh. Pictures of Christopher Robin's teddy bear are very similar to the early Farnell Alpha bears. The firm continued in business until the 1960s, when they finally closed their doors for the last time.

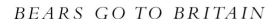

BEARS GO TO BRITAIN

Dean's Rag Book Company

One of the oldest surviving toy companies in Britain is Dean's Rag Book Company, founded by Henry Samuel Dean in 1903, which originally made indestructible rag books for small children. Its teddy bear production did not begin until the early days of the First World War in 1915 when the supply of imported German bears dried up and there was a huge gap in the domestic market.

Even in the middle of the war, the British public were still demanding teddy bears for their children to play with and Dean's obligingly diversified its business to satisfy consumers. The business flourished for many years – undoubtedly its most profitable and productive period was between the wars when its factory was based in Merton, South London.

By the end of the Second World War Dean's began to suffer increasing financial problems because the use of cheaper synthetic materials enabled other manufacturers to mass-produce teddy bears more cheaply. There was great competition in the toy market and in 1955 Dean's sold its Merton factory.

For the next 17 years, Dean's teddy bears were made at Rye in Sussex. After a merger in 1972, Dean's continued in business until in 1988 a new company was formed.

Since then, Dean's has started to re-establish its famous name in the world of teddy bears and is now producing replicas of its original bears as well as launching a completely new range of bears.

Left: A 1930s Dean's teddy bear.

Overleaf: A family portrait of a group of Chad Valley bears from the 1930s.

BEARS GO TO BRITAIN

The Johnson Brothers

Chad Valley success

In the early days of the 1820s two brothers, Joseph and Alfred Johnson, were running a printing business in Birmingham called Johnson Bros. Ltd. Nothing about Joseph or Alfred gave the slightest hint that their business would become world-famous for making toys. Only when the business moved to a new factory in 1897 did it register Chad Valley as its trademark, named after the Chad stream running nearby.

Right:An unusual Chad Valley bear from the 1930s in a jester style.

And that was the beginning of another teddy bear legend. The outbreak of war in 1914 prompted the enterprising Johnson family to respond to the ban on imports of German goods by producing their first range of teddy bears for the home market.

They quickly introduced a variety of teddy bears and other soft toys, expanding rapidly and establishing Chad Valley as a leading British manufacturer of delightful teddy bears. Everyone who bought toys for their children knew and trusted the Chad Valley name.

Eventually, more than half a century later in 1978, Chad Valley was taken over by Palitoy in 1978, after suffering a depression in its business, and ten years later in 1988 the famous Chad Valley name was adopted by Woolworths, another household favourite.

BEARS GO TO BRITAIN

Master Teddy
Chiltern's distinctive bear

Another British teddy bear business was quietly born in 1908. At first, Joseph Eisenmann's Chiltern Toy Works, based at Chesham in Buckinghamshire, only made dolls. But the shortage of teddy bears, the market leader among toys in 1915 in Britain, convinced Joseph that the business should expand and he launched his famous Master Teddy.

Left: A 1925 Chiltern teddy made with pink-coloured fur.

The amusing little bear's large googly eyes immediately caught on. His black stitched nose and little red tongue, poking out of his mouth gave him a distinctively different appearance. At first he was made with a little pink and white striped shirt with a white collar and a pair of trousers. Master Teddy was quite unlike any of the other bears made by Chiltern because he had no muzzle, was fully dressed and had no pads on his paws.

Chiltern became famous for its range of Hugmee bears in different designs and colours during the 1930s and the firm continued to make beautiful teddy bears throughout the years between the wars. There was a drop in production between 1939 and 1945, when the factory had to move from London to Amersham.

But after the war times were hard; there was increasingly fierce competition from new businesses, and the production of high-quality teddy bears, which had been under the direction of Joseph Eisenmann's son-in-law Leon Rees since 1919, eventually ceased altogether when the Amersham factory closed in 1960. Chiltern was completely taken over by Chad Valley in 1967 and eventually even the joint Chiltern/Chad Valley label disappeared.

Far left: Chiltern's famous Master Teddies made in 1915, with their smiling mouths and big googly eyes.

WARTIME BEARS

I heard the churcch bells hollowing out the sky,

Deep beyond deep, like never-ending stars,

And turned to Archibald, my safe old bear,

Whose woolen eyes looked sad or glad at me,

Whose ample forehead I could wet with tears,

Whose half-moon ears received my confidence,

Who made me laugh, who never let me down.

Summoned by Bells
John Betjeman

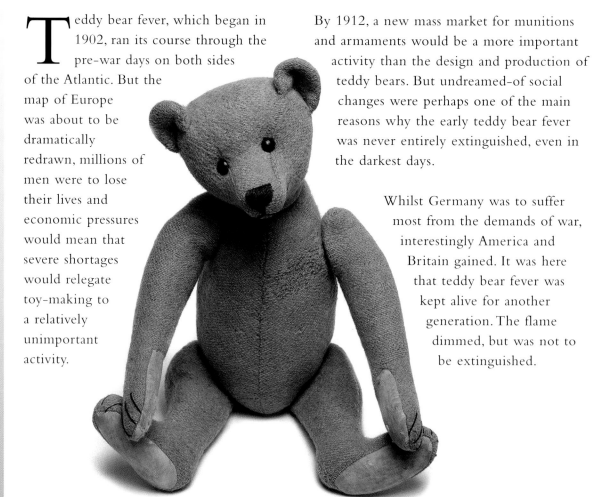

Right: A Steiff nettle bear from 1914. This bear was produced when there was a shortage of mohair; the fabric was a rough tweed type made from the fibre of nettle plants.

Teddy bear fever, which began in 1902, ran its course through the pre-war days on both sides of the Atlantic. But the map of Europe was about to be dramatically redrawn, millions of men were to lose their lives and economic pressures would mean that severe shortages would relegate toy-making to a relatively unimportant activity.

By 1912, a new mass market for munitions and armaments would be a more important activity than the design and production of teddy bears. But undreamed-of social changes were perhaps one of the main reasons why the early teddy bear fever was never entirely extinguished, even in the darkest days.

Whilst Germany was to suffer most from the demands of war, interestingly America and Britain gained. It was here that teddy bear fever was kept alive for another generation. The flame dimmed, but was not to be extinguished.

WARTIME BEARS

In Germany, Richard, Paul and Hugo Steiff had had to leave home and become part of the war machine. In the famous Steiff factory, output was disrupted because the government insisted that war munitions must be produced instead of children's toys. Additionally, foreign countries were refusing to buy German goods. Between 1914 and 1919, the name of Steiff lay almost dormant in the teddy bear world.

Far left: A 1915 Bing bear.

A ban on all imports from Germany at the start of the First World War in 1914 had an enormous impact on teddy bears. Throughout the world, whatever product had been made in Germany before the war was embargoed. Times were hard, labour and materials were in short supply everywhere. Toys of all kinds were low priorities when even sufficient food was difficult for most people to obtain.

But public demand for toys, especially teddy bears, did not suddenly disappear. Parents were still anxious to give their children soft toys as birthday presents – Christmas stockings still had to be filled. Even though austerity demanded that the war effort was to be put first, somehow, with ingenuity and enterprise, the British, French and Australians established themselves firmly as leaders in the market for the home-grown – and occasionally the home-made – teddy bear.

Left: A 1916 Farnell bear.

31

Battle of the Bears

Steiff and Bing go to war

In 1865, Ignaz and Adolf Bing had founded their own business in Nuremberg and called it Gebrüder Bing. Making kitchenware and tin, they were well established by about 1890 when they started to respond to an increasing demand for tin and enamelled toys for children. At the height of the teddy boom in 1907, they decided to make their first bears, and were immediately in competition with and litigated against by Steiff.

Above right: This Bing red tag was used from 1919 to 1927.

Right: This 1920s Bing bear has the metal tag on his wrist which was used between 1927 and 1932 to identify a Bing bear.

The problem was that the first Bing bears had a metal arrow attached to their ears. Set in a diamond shape, the initials GBN identified the teddy bear's origin as the factory of Gebrüder Bing. Steiff were furious, It was far too close to their own method of identification – the metal button in the ear. Bing changed their tactics and placed a metal button under the arm of each bear they produced. Steiff objected again. This time it was the button which annoyed them. Eventually, Bing were forced to remove the button and replace it with a label under the arm, printed with GBN.

BING'S MECHANICAL BEARS

By 1910, Bing had perfected the manufacture of the mechanical toy. This became sought after and made Bing famous in its own right. But the earliest Bing bears, made before the First World War, did closely resemble the Steiff bears and it was not until the 1920s that Bing redesigned their teddy bears with a longer snout, wide smile and distinctive muzzle stitching.

WARTIME BEARS

Litigation between Bing and Steiff was to be a constant feature of their rivalry in the early days. A charming hanging bear, which they brought out in 1910, provoked another lawsuit when Steiff claimed that it had been copied from their own similar Purzel Bär which they had made a year earlier. Equipped with a clockwork mechanism which wound the arms back, the bears had hooks on the ends of their paw pads. These hooks extended from metal rods in the arms and when the arms were wound back the bear performed somersaults which delighted children.

Other mechanical bears from this period included one with roller skates; another, fully dressed, on skis; a walking bear and a tumbling bear.

Bing's bears, with their very appealing little faces and specialised mechanical actions, were popular throughout the world but, by 1932, intense competition had forced them out of business.

Left: Bing's 1912 tumbling Bear.

Far left: A 1910 clockwork mechanical bear by Bing.

Below: Bing's fully clothed walking bear from 1915.

Overleaf: Three fabulous bears with very similar features; from left to right, a 1909 Steiff, a 1910 Bing and a 1910 Ideal bear.

Hermann Teddy Bear Dynasty

Just before the beginning of the war, in 1913, another German, Max Hermann, had started to make bears helped by his sister Adelheid and his brother Arthur. Together they used the trade name of the Johann Hermann Toy Factory. But their timing was unfortunate, and it was not until about 1920 that Max was able to found his own firm near to the then toy capital of the world, Sonneberg. The name Hermann Spielwaren is well known as one of the oldest family-owned manufacturers of teddy bears in Germany, forming with the Gebrüder Hermann (see below), what is known today as the Hermann Teddy Bear Dynasty.

The 1930s saw Hermann introduce the distinctive green triangle and the bear with a running dog label which is still used. The communist regime in East Germany after the Second World War threatened the survival of Max and his business. The family were forced to escape over the border to West Germany and were able to re-establish their factory in Coburg after an interim period between 1949 and 1953, during which their teddy bears were being produced in East and West Germany.

Another famous Hermann, Bernhard, began to supply the German home market with teddy bears from Sonneberg during the 1930s. He had four sons helping him in his factory, Horst, Hellmut, Artur and Werner – Gebrüder Hermann. The family-owned business had had links with America before the outbreak of war in 1939, and by 1948 Bernhard decided to move his business to the US zone of Germany. From their new factory in Hirschaid near Bambert, high-quality, traditionally made teddy bears continued to delight children even after the death of Bernhard in 1959, when the business was left to his three surviving sons. The distant cousins who still survive are all descended from the Sonneberg toymaker Johann Hermann.

The Impact of the First World War

Both the 1914-18 and 1939-45 wars challenged all teddy bear makers. Designs had to be adapted to desperate shortages of materials and skilled labour. Most of the earliest teddy bears were made with black boot-button eyes, made of wood with metal loops on the back which were similar to actual boot buttons of the period. Often these early toys were made using a form of hessian called burlap which was a coarse heavy fabric woven from jute or hemp. At first, many bears had a

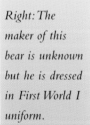

pronounced hump on the back – a design introduced by Steiff but quickly copied by many other manufacturers in the early years. Some of the first Steiff bears had metal rodded joints which ran through the entire body. Realistically moulded teddy bear noses were sometimes made using sealing wax – the sort which was produced to seal documents during the early 20th century. War changed all that. As already outlined, in the years between 1914 and 1919, overseas demand for German-made bears was almost wiped out. The concept of mass production was in its infancy and much work was done by hand. Factories were frequently commandeered for making munitions or uniforms by the British, as well as the Germans.

Despite these difficulties, materials were found to replace the traditional mohair fur and wood wool filling which was used to stuff the earliest bears, and some of these innovative alternatives remained in use after the fighting finally stopped.

Manufacturers were forced to adapt and innovate with surprising and far-reaching results. Although times were hard, money and labour were short and fortunes were made and lost, the incredible teddy bear survived and thrived.

Left: This quartet of Steiff bears show some of the different coloured mohairs used in manufacture.

Allied Bears

In Britain, 1914–18 proved a heaven-sent opportunity for teddy bear makers. They responded quickly, adapted, made do, and experimented with their own designs, restricted materials and relatively unskilled labour. By the 1920s Chiltern, Farnell and Chad Valley were well established and had acquired a reputation for imaginative, high-quality, sought-after teddy bears. In Britain, the traditional teddy bear's boot-button eyes had been gradually replaced by more realistic and colourful glass eyes as early as 1912.

A series of mascots dressed in uniforms of the allied forces proved especially popular. Made by Harwin & Co., who were established in 1914, the designs were similar to Steiff bears. Dorothy Harwin designed Ally Bear who was made in beautiful golden mohair plush, with boot-button eyes and a little shaved muzzle. Ally Bear was fully jointed and wore a perfect miniature replica of a khaki-coloured British army officer's uniform.

Right: This beautiful 1914 Harwin Ally Bear is complete with his original uniform.

Other small British firms were established during the war years when German bears were banned – Jungle

Toys, W. H. Jones and the British United Toy Manufacturing Co. were all names who took part in the real birth of the soft-toy industry, which grew in size, imagination and popularity throughout the 20th century.

TED

During the First World War Ted, a large Steiff bear, lived in Liverpool with two little girls who adored him. When German planes bombed the city, the two girls were taken to air-raid shelters for safety. Ted, although he was a German alien, went with them. After one of the sisters died of cancer while still very young, Ted stayed with the surviving sister, Esme, for the rest of her life. By the 1940s, Esme was busy with her own war effort, running a servicemen's canteen. And Ted always helped her, enjoying the company of young soldiers from all over the world. He was a favourite teatime companion throughout the war years, joined by his friend, belonging to Esme's neighbour's son who was called up to serve in the R.A.F. Although his owner was killed, Ted's friend remained with Esme, who was a kind and caring teddy bear lover all her life.

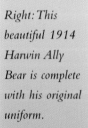

WARTIME BEARS

TUBBY

Tubby was another German Steiff bear who spent the war years in Britain as an enemy alien. In 1912, he was given to a little girl called Diana by her father when she was four years old. Diana adored him and she and Tubby were inseparable. They played together in the garden and shared donkey rides on the beach. Diana grew up to be a nurse after the end of the war, and Tubby went too, living with her in a London hospital. Eventually, Diana grew old and, when she was in very poor health, retired to a nursing home. Tubby stayed with her until she died.

BILLY BLUEGUM

The Australian koala

In Australia the koala bear, beloved by King Edward VII, rivalled the traditional teddy bear in popularity. In 1904, Billy Bluegum was created by Norman Lindsay, a famous Australian writer and illustrator, and was featured in a popular magazine. Several koala bears appeared on the market in Australia before 1914. During the war, Charles Jensen patented a jointed bear and in 1917 Fideston of Western Australia produced their first teddy bears for sale. In 1918, Norman Lindsay's book *The Magic Pudding* was published, Billy Bluegum was re-christened Bunyip Bluegum and Australian children were introduced to their own little bear.

Left: Tubby, a German Steiff bear.

EARLY SUPERSTAR BEARS

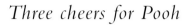

Three cheers for Pooh

For who?

For Pooh

Why, what did he do?

He saved his friend from a wetting

Three cheers for the wonderful Winnie the Pooh.

A. A. Milne

There is no doubt that the most famous bear of the period immediately after the First World War was the loveable, shy, hunny-eating Winnie the Pooh. He won the hearts of children and their parents for ever and has been absorbed into the fabric of childhood.

Three Cheers for Pooh!
A. A. Milne's timeless classic

The appearance of Winnie the Pooh – a bear of very little brain – in the 1920s was one of the earliest hints that the teddy bear could become a superstar. The "tubby little cubby all stuffed with fluff", as a later song put it, won millions of hearts and was to become world famous.

A. A. Milne's *When We Were Very Young*, a collection of poems, was first published by Methuen in 1924. His subsequent stories *The House at Pooh Corner* and poems, which were inspired by the teddy bear given to his small son, Christopher Robin as a birthday present in 1921, achieved astounding popularity. Originally, Winnie the Pooh was an Alpha Farnell bear bought from Harrods and christened "Teddy" or "Bear" by his small owner. The grown ups knew him more grandly as "Edward Bear".

As Christopher Robin grew bigger, he decided that it was time his bear had a "proper" name. In fact, the name Pooh belonged to a swan which Christopher Robin had found when he was staying in Arundel, Sussex. "Winnie" was the name of a North American bear – once a mascot to the Canadian Brigade during the First World War – which Christopher Robin had fallen madly in love with on a trip to the London Zoo.

Although in his first book of poems A. A. Milne wrote about a bear, it was not given the name Winnie the Pooh until he was drafting his second book at the end of 1925. As it began Christopher Robin was coming down the stairs, trailing his bear behind him.

Ernest Shepard, who was commissioned to illustrate the stories, brought the little boy

EARLY SUPERSTAR BEARS

and his bear to life with his wonderful drawings, many of them actually based on Christopher Robin's own soft toys, although the model for Winnie the Pooh was actually his own son's Steiff bear, Growler. Bumping down the stairs, Winnie the Pooh made his first appearance, and another teddy bear legend was born.

The original drawings were done in black and white. When he was in his nineties, Ernest Shepard was commissioned to add colour wash and the originals can now be seen at the Victoria and Albert Museum in London.

The story of Winnie the Pooh and Christopher Robin has delighted and amused adults as well as children since the mid-1920s. Today there can hardly be a household that does not have at least one Winnie the Pooh replica or story.

Who could fail to fall in love with Pooh? His friends Piglet, Tigger, Kanga and Roo, Eeyore and Rabbit – not forgetting Small (short for Very Small Beetle) and all Rabbit's friends and relations – were all Christopher Robin's friends too.

Left: An Alpha Farnell bear; one of these was owned by Christopher Robin and became the inspiration behind A. A. Milne's Winnie the Pooh.

Teddy B and Teddy G

The first and most famous fictional American bears were the two delightful Roosevelt Bears. Stories about Teddy B (brown) and Teddy G (grey) were published to the enormous delight of American children in 1905. Written by Seymour Eaton, they prompted some of the earliest character teddy bears to be made which helped these charming stories to come to life. Children could have their very own Roosevelt Bears to love and play with.

Rupert Hits the Papers

The nearest a bear ever came to resembling a human child was Rupert Bear, created by Mary Tourtel as a comic strip character in 1920. Mary Tourtel was a children's book illustrator whose husband was an editor on the *Daily Express*. Rupert Bear was her brainwave. He was an immediate success in the newspaper and the comic strip stories, books and annuals which followed were translated into so many languages that Rupert, the most lovable of little bears, was famous throughout the world.

The little bear in his red jumper, yellow-checked trousers and scarf, together with his friends Algy and Bill Badger was a household name during the 1930s. By 1932 he had collected so many fans that a Rupert League was devoted to him.

Rupert's arch-rival, Teddy Tail was another character of the 1930s who appeared in the *Daily Mail*, but he never acquired the same level of popularity as Rupert.

Right: An array of Rupert toys, books and paraphernalia.

Thousands of families followed Rupert's adventures throughout the 1930s and 40s. Although his image has been reproduced in a wide variety of forms – books, plates, biscuit and sweet tins, wooden puppets and postcards – it was not until the 1960s that soft-toy versions of Rupert Bear appeared.

In 1970 an animated series was screened on British TV and in 1984 a Rupert video was released. In Britain, Pedigree Soft Toys and Merrythought produced their own authentic versions of Rupert Bear.

During the 1990s, Merrythought brought out their own "limited" edition of 10,000 Rupert Bears, accompanied by his lifelong chum Bill Badger. In America the company Real Soft Toys created their own Rupert

teddy bears for children. The Northampton firm of Burbank Toys had produced a small number of Rupert Bear teddies in the 1960s, fully dressed in classic Rupert clothes with black and brown eyes and soft stuffing.

When Mary Tourtel retired, she was succeeded as Rupert's illustrator by Alfred Bestall who carried on working at the comic strip drawings well into his nineties, finally retiring in the 1980s.

Blinky Bill

Ask any Australian to tell you about Blinky Bill, an Australian literary koala bear. Dorothy Wall created this cheeky little character whose stories were published by the Australian Whitman Publishing Company, starting in 1935. Blinky Bill became an instant favourite down under. Morella Fur Toys, an Australian business, made a few jointed Blinky Bill koala bears from kangaroo hide, filled with sawdust. Unfortunately these little bears did not stand the test of time and it was not until the 1970s that soft-toy Blinky Bills were made under copyright to Angus and Robertson.

Baloo Sings for Disney

Earlier in the 20th century, Rudyard Kipling had created his own bear, Baloo, who was also to be catapulted to fame with Disney's *Jungle Book* movie in the 1960s with his irresistible song 'Bare Necessities' and his trademark prickly pear.

THE ROARING 20s

I wish I had a Teddy Bear,

To sit upon my knee.

I'd take him with me everywhere,

To cuddle up with me.

I'd scorn young men,

No lover then

My lot in life should share

They all might go to Jericho

If I'd a Teddy Bear

Pelissier's Follies, 1909

*Far right:
Farnell's label for
its Alpha bears,
stitched to the
foot pad of a
bear.*

By 1923, Chiltern had introduced its Hugmee teddy bears and the next year it officially registered the Chiltern toys trademark. In Germany, the toymaker Gebrüder Süssenguth made its famous Peter Bear in 1925, the same year that J. K. Farnell registered its Alpha trademark in Britain.

*Right: A 1925
Chiltern
Hugmee bear.*

In France, the firm of Fadap was established in 1923 and that year it produced its first teddy bears. Fadap (it stands for Fabrication Artistic d'Animaux en Peluche) was based in Divonne-les-Bains. Its earliest bears have delightful pear-shaped bodies and they are

THE ROARING 20s

tubby, with long arms and thick paws, irresistible with their lovely little upturned noses. Their black boot-button eyes, four claws and realistic voice box ensured that these bears took France by storm. The Second World War resulted in drastically reduced production and in 1978 the firm finally closed down.

Left: A hard stuffed Fadap bear, typical of French bears. This one has a lovely curious expression on his face and still retains the maker's button in his ear.

Pintel et Fils

But the very first French bear manufacturer was Pintel et Fils. As early as 1913, Marcel Pintel had started to make a range of stuffed toys for his father's Paris-based business. He was young, bright and full of energy, with plenty of enthusiasm and new ideas. Young Marcel Pintel was also very competitive and determined to make the toys he designed even better than those already on the market. His very first mechanical tumbling clown bear actually appeared in the trade catalogue in 1911.

Although the First World War slowed down the rate of production, Marcel Pintel spent what time he could developing a completely new range of toys including a stuffed mohair bear which appeared in 1920. With typical French flair, the popular Pintel bears were delicate, with substantial filling and elegant tapering limbs. Demand was so great that part of their production had to be outsourced to newer toymakers.

Right: A lovely bear by the very First French manufacturer, Pintel et Fils.

Joy Toys

Australia joins in bear mania

Throughout the 1920s the teddy bear industry was really booming. On the other side of the world, the Australians were in on the act too. An imaginative and energetic firm called Joy Toys was set up during the early 1920s which specialised in making beautiful soft toys – and, of course, these included a range of teddy bears. In the next 40 years Joy toys was to make over 50,000 bears.

Joy Toy bears were soon being made in many styles. At first they were fully jointed and made from English mohair filled with excelsior. This was a soft mixture of long thin wood shavings, otherwise known as wood wool, and was the most commonly used material for stuffing toy bears at this time. In shape, the Australian bears were very like the German bears of that time with their distinctive slim bodies and limbs.

The actual Joy Toy trademark did not appear until the 1930s, by which time the neck was no longer jointed so that the head was immovable. These later teddy bears were more like the British bears in shape; many of them had unusual pointed upturned front paws, and kapok – a lightweight, silky fibre derived from a seed pod – was being used for stuffing.

Colour and Music
Novelty bears

After the end of the First World War, the depression years saw the rise of a range of novelty bears – some of them amusing, others stretching the imagination to its limit. From the earliest days the manufacturers of teddy bears were producing small novelties. Often a growler or squeaker mechanism was included – one of the amusing extras.

Before long designers began to think of even more exciting innovations. In Germany, musical bears were very popular. Steiff and Bing both became famous for their mechanical walking, dancing and tumbling bears.

Left: A delightful pair of very rare Steiff dancing bears from the 1920s.

Bears were incorporated into many other products – bags, purses, hand muffs and night-dress cases – many of them produced specially for children, although they were also popular as fun gifts for adults. An American bear had "Electric Eyes" which actually lit up, and a whistling teddy bear appeared. For very small children, teddy bear novelties included hot water bottles and rattles. Many of these novelties were made at home by hand or by small businesses, which disappeared without trace over the years.

Far left: A 1920s Bing bear with a long shaved muzzle and beautifully shaggy golden mohair.

THE ROARING 20s

Right: A 1920s musical Pappe Moritz bear. Moritz was a German manufacturer who also made a somersaulting bear similar to Steiff's, as well as clown bears and coloured art silk bears.

Left: Earlier
novelty bears
included a range
of muzzle bears
such as this
1910 Steiff,
complete with his
original leather
muzzle.

Petsy Bear was first introduced by Steiff in Germany in 1928 and the use of dual-plush – a new kind of mohair with the ends painted in a second colour and known as tipped mohair – became very popular with many other teddy bear makers. Steiff still had the resources to produce innovative ideas in design and materials which were quickly copied by their rivals.

Right: Petsy Bear, introduced by Steiff in 1928. Petsy has blue glass googly eyes and wired ears.

Chiltern and Farnell were quick to respond to the mood in Britain at the end of the 1920s with the use of artificial silk plush – a new man-made fibre which could be dyed in various colours

Right: This colourful German bear's maker is unknown but he has a musical bellows movement.

German manufacturers in the late-1920s combined colour with music to produce a range of brightly coloured long-haired bears playing a variety of different tunes. Several designs of musical bears were available and made lovely novelty gifts for adults as well as children. The musical mechanism worked by means of a bellows movement in the bear's tummy – very simply operated by squeezing.

Merrythought

A Yorkshire partnership set up in 1919 between W. G. Holmes and G. H. Laxton eventually became one of the leading British teddy bear manufacturers of the century. A small spinning mill in Oakworth soon proved too small for the new business which took over a weaving factory in Huddersfield in 1920. Two directors were taken on: A. C. Janisch, who had been sales director for J. K. Farnell, and C. J. Rendle, who had organised toy production for Chad Valley.

This was to prove a winning team. With first-hand experience of two of the leading teddy bear manufacturers of the time, the company's next few years were spent consolidating and expanding.

By 1930 the company was ready to rent larger premises when it moved to Coalbrookdale in Shropshire. The same year it registered the Merrythought Ltd name which it took from the 17th-century English word for wishbone. This symbol of good luck still features on the label and button of Merrythought teddy bears.

It was not long before Merrythought became one of the leading British manufacturers of soft toys. In 1936 it introduced Bobby Bruin, a distinctive little bear quite unlike the designs which were to capture the hearts of so many children in later years. During the 1930s the Bingie range of bears, dressed and undressed, followed the exceptionally successful Highlander Bingie which went on sale in 1925.

Right: A group of musical Steiff clown bears produced in the 1920s.

Bears Everywhere!

Bears for fun appeared as early as the Victorian era. In 1860, Raphael Tuck, who was a Prussian business man, introduced German printing methods to the production of postcards and greetings cards in Britain. At this early stage, bears were drawn as real grizzlies and not our familiar teddy bears. Tuck also produced embossed cards which proved extremely popular – and he could boast Queen Victoria as one of his customers.

Paper was, of course, a perfect medium for the teddy bear. The 20th-century teddy bear craze immediately hit the greetings and

postcard business worldwide. Birthday and Christmas cards for children were attractive and topical, creating another new market. Children's writers soon began to write stories about teddy bears and books which featured bears became very popular with children in America and Britain, .

Although the earliest children's bear books featured the grizzly bear, writers very quickly adapted and were inspired to write wonderful adventure stories with teddy bear heroes. Many of these were translated into other languages. Literary teddy bear include Seymour Eaton's Teddy B and

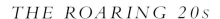

THE ROARING 20s

Teddy G; the traditional folk tale Goldilocks and the Three Bears; Mary Tourtel's Rupert Bear; Michael Bond's Paddington Bear; Dorothy Walls' Blinky Bill and, of course, the famous Winnie the Pooh.

Seymour Eaton's real name was Paul Piper and he created the two Roosevelt Bears in 1905. The stories were published in 20 leading American newspapers as a series before they appeared in book form. The two bears in the early stories are very similar to the real American grizzly bear. But by the time the second series was published, Eaton was actually calling his two bears "teddy bears". The first volume of stories was illustrated by Floyd Campbell, while the illustrator for the next two books was R. K. Culver and the final volume had pictures by Francis P. Wightman and William K. Sweeney. In America the Roosevelt Bears were enormously popular, so much so that Teddy B and Teddy G outfits were made and sold to children for their very own teddy bears.

Sheet music with bear songs and marches appeared. Jigsaw puzzles and games, cardboard cut-out bears which could be dressed in different outfits, drawings and paintings all celebrated the arrival of the teddy bear.

Between 1907 and 1911 there were more than 40 songs which featured teddy bears. The most popular of all was written in 1907 by the American composer John Bratton and is still with us today 'The Teddy Bears' Picnic'. By the 1930s this catchy tune had been given words by the songwriter Jimmy Kennedy and played on the radio to enchant a whole new generation of British children.

One of the most popular water colour painters of bears was Leigh Beavis West, whose classic portraits of teddy bears are collected by bear and art lovers and are still reproduced endlessly on gift products and stationery.

Left: A delightful pair of 1920s Steiff bears.

THE ROARING 20s

The Morning Walk.

Right: A 1930s postcard.

The postage stamp has carried bears as a symbol worldwide in various forms. Special editions are often issued and it is possible to find stamps with lovely illustrations of black bears, polar bears, literary bears as well as teddy bears. Rupert Bear, the Three Bears and Paddington Bear have all been featured by Britain's Royal Mail between 1989 and 1994.

Seymour Eaton produced many postcards on which Teddy B and Teddy G appeared. Parents loved to have photographic postcards of their children posing with their bears and some German cards of the early 1900s show just how large these early teddy bears actually were.

Even before teddy bear fever hit the world, bears were popular enough to be reproduced in many different mediums. The early Black Forest wooden bears were a reproduction of the real bear – whilst the early Clifford Berryman cartoons marked the very beginning of the age of the teddy bear.

Of course, the commercial potential of the teddy bear was not lost on manufacturers of china and porcelain who incorporated them into many products in various designs.

At the end of the 19th century, there were some beautifully carved wooden bears available in Germany and Switzerland, many of them connected with smoking – matchbox holders, ashtrays, pipe holders and smoker's tables. Accessories for dressing tables and desks were made and often these were engraved and sold as souvenirs.

Children's china – mugs, cups, bowls and plates or dolls' tea services – was made in Germany and England and considerable quantities were sold. Jean Allen was an English china decorator who painted many different plates between the 1930s and the 1960s which featured bears. Around 1900 some delightful little German bisque bears were available in sets and some of these still survive, over a century later.

Another firm, with the registered trademark "Ealontoys", was established in 1914 by the famous suffragette Sylvia Pankhurst. Originally known as the East London Federation Toy Factory, it produced many novelties, including a delightful teddy bear hot water bottle cover. In 1948, the firm changed its name to Ealontoys Ltd.

Left: An early postcard dating back to 1909.

Heirloom Bears

Sometimes it is possible to identify bears which have a recorded family history, and this is very exciting because it brings the bear to life in a unique way.

BILL

A rare German Steiff bear, named Bill, with a long curly mohair coat, was very fortunate to receive an excellent education. In 1907 he was given to a little boy called Reginald for his first birthday. In 1908 Reginald's brother Esmond was born and later the two boys had a little sister called Althea.

The two little boys cherished Bill and took him everywhere with them. In 1919 he went to Harrow school and in 1922 to Eton. He finished his education at both Oxford and Cambridge universities. Eventually, Althea, who had been born in 1917, was allowed to care for him and to the boys' horror she insisted on dressing him up in clothes and taking him out in a doll's pram.

Eventually, in 1925, Bill was allowed to retire. But in 1957, he was given to Esmond's grandchildren and travelled everywhere with them until 1972 when he was given to a collector and at last allowed to take his place in teddy bear history.

TEDDY GIRL

Other historic teddy bears include one who survived the sinking of the *Titanic* and a beautiful early Steiff cinnamon-coloured teddy bear called Teddy Girl who changed hands at auction in London for a world-record price.

Teddy Girl had originally been Teddy Boy, and was first given to the brother of an army officer, Colonel Henderson. When his daughter received him as a present she gave Teddy Boy a dress to wear and re-named him Teddy Girl. Teddy Girl travelled the world, and eventually settled in Australia, having been the lifelong companion of Colonel Henderson and the inspiration for his famous collection of 500 teddy bears.

TARQUIN

Tarquin was originally an RAF mascot bear. During the Second World War he had belonged to an RAF squadron. After the war, his first owners were untraceable and, in spite of photographs appearing of Tarquin wearing his flying suit adorned with RAF badges, large wellington boots, rakish silk cravat, radio ear-phones and leather helmet, no-one ever claimed him. He was eventually bought at auction in Lincolnshire and given as a present to the novelist Jack Higgins, a collector of Second World War memorabilia.

ROSEMOUSE

The invading German forces had nearly reached Paris and, with their possessions packed onto carts, entire families fled for their lives. These were dangerous times – but for a small boy there was the hint of adventure and the tingle of excitement as well as fear of the enemy.

In 1932 a little French boy, whose name I do not know, had been given a teddy bear for his birthday. The most popular waltz tune at that time was called Rosemouse – and that was what the small boy decided to call his beloved teddy bear. In the years before

the outbreak of war the pair were inseparable. But shortly after the war began the family, fearing for their lives, were forced to leave their home.

During the escape, Rosemouse was treated with great care by the small boy's parents and this puzzled him a great deal. It was only much later, when they reached safety, that he discovered the truth. Rosemouse had carried the entire family fortune to safety in his tummy

Left: A black, centre-seam Steiff bear made in 1912. These black bears were often referred to as Titanic bears as England was mourning the sinking of the ship Titanic and the black bears reflected the sombre mourning mood of the country.

BEARS OF THE 1930s

Take my dolls,

Pull my hair,

Take my dog,

I don't care

But never take

My Teddy Bear

Anonymous

French Bears

Before the Second World War several French manufacturers made a variety of bears. With typical French flair, these were often made of materials other than the traditional mohair plush. Thiennot, Faye and Alfa Paris were among the best-known toymakers and in the 1930s Faye made a tiny blue bear only about 12 inches long, with metal rods for his arms and legs.

Another unusual 1930s French bear was made of white flannel material with red cotton pads and red cotton ear linings. With his barrel-shaped body and unjointed head, this large teddy bear had a very sad mouth, which characterised many of the French bears made between the wars.

Right: A bear by the French manufacturer, Pintel et Fils.

Until 1919, Emile Thiennot had worked for Marcel Pintel. He then decided to set up on his own and formed a toy-making company called Le Jouet Champenois. He quickly became very successful and in 1920 one of his teddy bears won a medal in a French competition.

The Second World War put a stop to most of the teddy bear production in France and although there was a revival in the early 1950s – there were more than 25 manufacturers listed at the 1951 Salon de Jouet – the French toy fair – many of the smaller firms later went into liquidation. Pintel and Fadap were two manufacturers which had survived the war and continued to make teddy bears.

Left: An Alpha Farnell bear with a small artist's bear.

British Bears of the 30s

By the mid-1930s, Merrythought had grown into the largest soft-toy manufacturer in the UK. Expansion was rapid during the 1920s and in 1932 the company had rented even larger factory space from the nearby iron foundry at Ironbridge in Shropshire, where the staff had grown to nearly 200. Electric motors had been installed so that power-driven sewing machines could be used. Storage sheds contained large quantities of stuffing, crates and packing cases whilst the completed and packed teddy bears were kept in the stockrooms.

When the Second World War broke out the success of this thriving company was interrupted. The factory was taken over by the government to produce maps and the space was used for storage of plywood, gaberdine and velour fabric.. At a makeshift temporary factory in nearby Wellington, a few toys continued to be made with a skeleton staff and very restricted materials.

Right: This 1930s Merrythought bear is typical of the bears made at that time, covered in curly mohair and stuffed with kapok. He has a celluloid button in his ear.

Right: One of the earliest Merrythought labels from 1930. These were usually embroidered onto a foot.

The chief designer for Merrythought was Florence Atwood, who died in 1949. She created her designs from the ideas of several other artists as well as her own, and in 1939 was inspired by the arrival of Ming the giant panda at London Zoo to create the very first Merrythought panda bear.

BEARS OF THE 1930s

In 1946, just after the end of the war, the River Severn flooded and, disastrously, all Merrythought's pre-war samples and many of their remaining supplies were destroyed. When the production manager C. J. Rendle died in 1949, the founder's son, Trayton Holmes, joined the company.

Left: A 1950s Pixie bear of Stourbridge.

CASUALTIES OF WAR

The lean years of the 1930s and 1940s forced many of the smaller English teddy bear manufacturers out of business. In 1937 W. H. Jones, which had been one of the pioneers of British soft-toy manufacturing, ceased production. The Teddy Toy Company, which had started at the outbreak of the First World War and become very famous for its Softanlite teddies during the 1920s and 30s, eventually wound up its business in 1951. Other firms such as Pixie Toys of Stourbridge and Invicta Toys of London managed to survive the war but were sadly forced to close in the 1950s and 60s.

Far left: A 1930s Bingie Bear made by Merrythought. He is very rare, being clothed in his original costume.

61

MATERIAL CHANGES

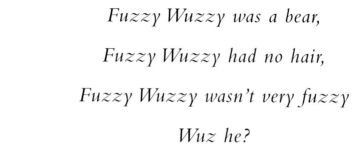

Fuzzy Wuzzy was a bear,

Fuzzy Wuzzy had no hair,

Fuzzy Wuzzy wasn't very fuzzy

Wuz he?

Traditional

The Second World War marked the beginning of a period when materials were in shorter supply than ever before, which was to have a decisive effect on the manufacture of the teddy bear.

Most bears made before about 1945 were made from silk mohair plush. This came from the wool of the angora goat. During the 1920s dual-coloured mohair plush was extremely popular. Until the outbreak of war in 1939 a few bears were made from an early synthetic material – rayon silk plush – and gradually the new synthetic fibres became more common. These synthetic fibres are harder to the touch and shinier than natural mohair.

At the beginning of the teddy bear craze, most German bears were stuffed with a material called excelsior or wood wool, a wood-based stuffing made from very fine wood shavings which had been commonly used for packing. A few bears were stuffed with kapok, which is a soft silky fibre, and many bears made in the early days contained a mixture of the two materials. Between 1920 and 1930 both English and German bears were often stuffed only with kapok as this feels both softer and lighter. After the end of the Second World War teddy bears usually contained synthetic machine-washable stuffing which is the lightest and softest of all.

Right: A beautiful 1920s Steiff bear.

MATERIAL CHANGES

Early German Steiff black bears had black boot-button eyes set against circles of red felt. The boot-button eyes were made from metal or wood and were usually stitched to the head or attached by hooks or wires. After about 1914, glass eyes were used more commonly. These were always attached by wire shanks. Variations on the classic boot-button eyes included enamelled metal eyes, moving googly eyes and painted clear-glass eyes. During the 1950s, plastic eyes were the order of the day as these were much safer for children.

A great many of the early bears had hand-stitched embroidered noses. Different makers used different methods and both the shape of the nose and the type of stitching varied from maker to maker. After 1950, rubber noses, which looked very realistic, were introduced. Although many modern bears are still made with plastic noses, the noses of collector's bears are still made with hand stitching.

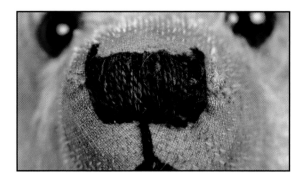

Teddy bear paws vary a great deal in their shape and size. The materials they are made from depend on the type of bear, the period and the manufacturer. Mostly, felt was used for paws of the earliest bears, in brown, cream or beige. Sometimes black bears had matching paws. The paws were almost always reinforced with card or fabric to give the fragile felt more strength. Throughout the whole of the 20th century, leather had been used for paws and during the 1930s, cotton or woven cotton and velveteen became increasingly popular. A cheaper alternative, called rexine – a type of oilcloth material – was sometimes used for pads from the early 1930s.

Far left: The eyes of an early German Steiff black bear; boot button eyes set against circles of red felt.

Above and below left: The different stitching to be found on bear noses and a rubber nose on a 1960s Chiltern bear.

Left: Teddy bear paws vary a great deal in their shape and size. The materials they are made from depend on the type of bear.

Right: This 1930s Chiltern Hugmee bear is made of luxurious shaggy mohair and has a typical shaved muzzle with a dstinctive nose stitched vertically in long upward end stitches. Chiltern bears made at this time had either clear glass eyes or brown glass eyes, like this one.

*Left: Musical
bears were made
by many
manufacturers.
Some German
makers
specialised in
musical and
other novelty
bears during the
1920s and '30s;
and like these
two, of unknown
origin, they used
vibrant colours
and tipped
mohair.*

MATERIAL CHANGES

The severe disruption of the thriving European teddy bear industry between 1939 and 1945 meant that, although some companies were still able to produce a limited quota, they were forced to use inferior materials. Although natural fibres were still used after the war, a great many teddy bears were made from synthetic materials for the mass market. Post-war bears, although made from less traditional materials, were made in many original designs which were often based on stories, films and cartoons.

Social and technological change after the war drastically changed the face of the soft-toy industry. Many traditional manufacturers had to cease production in the face of competition from the cheap mass-produced toys from the Far East. By the late 1960s it seemed as though the traditional teddy bear was doomed.

Restore or Leave?

Right: A Merrythought, 'Cheeky' bear in poor shape.

In some families, teddy bears have been carefully kept and handed down from generation to generation. Old bears need care and attention – they are, after all, antiques and can be valuable. Although simple repairs can be done at home, a bear which needs restoring should be cared for by an expert. Professional teddy bear restorers are usually listed in teddy bear magazines which are published worldwide.

There are lots and lots of unidentified vintage teddy bears around still whose origin is uncertain and may never be known. Often, though, it is possible for the date they were made to be discovered, and certain

characteristics can point to the country of origin. Although the metal buttons used by Steiff and Bing identified these bears easily, parents often removed them for safety and many older teddy bears only had paper tags which were taken off before the children were given the toys.

Many old teddy bears have suffered from the energetic love and attention they have received from several generations of children. They may lose their stitching, have noses and ears pulled off or even lose their limbs. Many mothers have tried to repair the damage – sometimes with the only materials which were to hand at the time. The result is often odd glass eyes, mismatching paw pads and the wrong type and colour of thread used for stitching. A professional teddy bear restorer can repair almost any bear correctly and many will give advice on how this can be done as well as being able to date and identify most old bears.

MATERIAL CHANGES

Sometimes a teddy bear is in a very bad condition and cannot be properly restored. If the fabric has become dry and brittle, it may crumble away when it is stitched because it has rotted. Glue can be hard to remove if it has been used for amateur repairs. If a nose needs replacing and the material around the muzzle has become too weak, sometimes a matching colour mohair can be found and a new muzzle set in so that the nose and mouth can be stitched in again.

Left: The same Merrythought bear after restoration.

MATERIAL CHANGES

If the body and pads have holes these can be patched – and if the rest of the mohair on the bear is still good the patched areas may not show too much. If the teddy bear shows signs of great age and is too dilapidated, then a transplant may be the only answer.

Each teddy bear has a unique face and this is usually the charming feature which first catches the eye of a potential owner. A teddy bear parade of unidentified vintage bears might include a 1930s bear with a thick soft golden mohair coat and clear glass eyes; a First World War red boy with limbs which have been replaced; a girl teddy with a flat face and short limbs; another made after the Second World War using Utility cotton plush; and a small French bear with the typical characteristics of ears which do not match the material of the body and limbs. Many French bears were of a very basic design and made using cotton and wool materials.

Older teddy bears made in America during the 1930s can be spotted by their barrel-shaped bodies, distinctive nose stitching.

Right: An American bear with distinctive barrel-shaped body and nose stitching.

bright-coloured short mohair fur and cotton paw pads. Often these bears have been dressed in modern clothes to protect them from wear and damage.

Battered-looking bears are often very appealing indeed. They may have a twisted nose, odd eyes or lopsided ears. If you find and fall for one of these bears, you could probably have it successfully restored. It will almost certainly respond to cleaning and mending without losing the characteristics which endeared it to you at first sight. Stuffing can be replaced, new or repaired pads can be added, eyes replaced and noses re-stitched or mended. Gentle, thorough cleaning will restore your little bear to its original handsome self.

With a much-loved family bear, though, the thought of restoring may be just too much. Altering the original character of the bear may destroy the bear's family history and sometimes, if your bear has eyes which are too large or unmatching these features somehow give it its true character and complement its personality. If you love it as it is, even if it is not quite right, it would be a shame to change it.

MATERIAL CHANGES

If you consider having a vintage bear restored, it is important to stop and consider whether it will be a success. Often a bear can be in such a bad way that the effort of restoration may be both expensive and disappointing. If an early Steiff or Farnell bear is a good example of its period, then it should certainly be restored by a professional because these are valuable bears and any money spent will add to the value. Usually the fabric used to make these bears was of such high quality that it will respond to careful and sympathetic restoration.

Left: A chiltern bear in a poor state (above) and the restored bear (below).

If you have a bear which is simply an elderly cherished friend, made of lesser-quality material, the cost of restoration may not be worthwhile. But some people, even though the cost of restoration far exceeds the value of the teddy bear, still have repairs done professionally rather than lose their beloved bear forever.

A NEW AGE FOR BEARS

Picnic time for teddy bears

The little teddy bears

Are having a wonderful time today...

Sooty (and Soo)

In the 1950s, Sooty and his friend Soo were two of the most popular children's TV characters. British comedian Harry Corbett's simple glove puppets first appeared on British TV in 1952. Their conjuring tricks and silly antics were so successful with their young audiences that they were given their own TV series which became one of the longest-running children's shows ever.

The first series of shows was called *Teddy Bear Magician* and at the end of each show, Sooty played 'The Teddy Bear's Picnic' on a xylophone. Sooty, his dog friend Sweep and Soo created havoc for Harry Corbett who was always their victim – which delighted the children who watched their shows.

Various companies manufactured the Sooty xylophone but it was Chad Valley that made the glove puppets for which they held the rights for many years. In about 1960, the Royal National Institution for the Blind adopted the enormously popular Sooty as their mascot and large collecting boxes were made showing Sooty holding a box and his famous magic wand.

Sooty fans bought a wide variety of games and novelties during the 1950s and 60s and eventually other companies began making Sooty merchandise which continued until the 1980s.

An old lady had sold the very first Sooty glove puppet to Harry Corbett on Blackpool pier. Corbett took the puppet home and blackened the nose and ears with soot – which is where he got his name. Over a thousand Sooty puppet have been worn out since then.

Nookie Bear and Others

Another entertaining little bear was called Nookie – he belonged to the ventriloquist Roger de Courcey and was a big hit when he first appeared on British TV. Nookie and Roger became very famous via their regular TV appearances and several shows at the London Palladium. Nookie bear became one of the UK's best-selling toys.

Across the Atlantic, from about 1970, Smokey Bear was made by R. Dakin & Co., under licence from the "Co-operative Fire Prevention Programme". One version was made of plastic and had moveable arms; another was made of plush.

By the 1960s and 70s many teddy bears clearly had star quality and a few became so

A NEW AGE FOR BEARS

famous that they were recognised in many countries around the world. Their stories, often originating from a cartoon, were written in many different languages and became incredibly popular. The world of film and television catapulted the shy hunny-loving Winnie the Pooh to instant stardom when Walt Disney bought the rights in 1964 and introduced him in his own animated pictures. From 1966 Pooh and his friends Piglet, Tigger, Kanga, Roo, Eeyore and Rabbit were as well known as Disney's own Mickey Mouse of the 1930s.

In America many of the biggest teddy bear manufacturers made their own versions of Pooh and his friends. Mountains of other merchandise appeared for sale – puzzles, games, books and other toys.

Left: A cotton plush Sooty.

A NEW AGE FOR BEARS

An American bear-maker, Agnes Brush, was ahead of the Disney game. In about 1952 she got permission from Steven Slesinger, who held the copyright from A. A Milne until Disney bought it in 1964, and made her own delightful version of Winnie the Pooh. Gund produced a small Piglet.

Merrythought made a complete set of Kanga, Roo (who fits into Kanga's pocket), Piglet and Eeyore and Pooh in the 1960s which were based on the Disney cartoon rather than the original Ernest Shepard drawings. Very much earlier, in 1935,

A NEW AGE FOR BEARS

Merrythought had produced a bear with a button in his ear wearing a red jersey to make him look like Winnie the Pooh.

In 1960, the first book written in Latin ever to reach the New York bestseller list was a Latin version of Milne's *Winnie the Pooh* story, entitled *Winnie Ille Pu*. The story was translated into Latin by Alexander Lenard, a Hungarian doctor.

Left: Pooh and Piglet, made by Merrythought in the 1960s.

A NEW AGE FOR BEARS

Wendy Boston
The revolutionary washable bear

The traditional bear underwent a revolution after the Second World War when Wendy Boston created the first safe, hygienic, washable teddy bear. This is what changed the face of the soft-toy market for ever.

In 1945 Wendy Boston and her husband Ken founded their business, making soft toys in a small shop in South Wales. At first they had a staff of only three people. Wendy designed her own bears and Ken did the marketing and company management. Within two years they had a staff of 16 and were making a range of traditional animals in addition to teddy bears. Some of the animals were made in mohair and were fully jointed.

Just after the war in England toys were in very short supply and it was not long before the business was selling everything it could make. Wendy and Ken decided to expand and they found and opened a factory in Abergavenny in 1948. The staff grew to 30 and Wendy decided that it was time to stop merely responding to demand – time to innovate and compete vigorously with other manufacturers. She realised, well ahead of her time, that attitudes towards toys were changing. Parent were becoming more safety-conscious and concerned with bits that could be swallowed or sharp items that might scratch their children.

First Wendy invented the locked-in safe plastic eye. Then she developed her ideas further so that by the mid-50s the very first foam-filled, nylon-covered teddy bear was test-marketed. It was very successful indeed. The little bear was filled with foam

chippings and could be washed and even put through the mangle without any loss of shape or softness. Hoover finally rigorously tested the first bear and issued a certificate which recommended that it should be given a gentle wash and spin dry in their machines.

The company changed its name to Wendy Boston Playsafe Toys Ltd in 1960, advertising itself as "The first firm in the world to make a complete range of washable sponge-filled nylon toys with moulded screw-locked eyes."

In addition Wendy Boston made a range of traditional jointed and unjointed mohair bears which were exported all over the world. By 1964, it was claimed that she had 28 per cent of the entire market. But her wonderful new innovations, which ensured safety above all, added enormously to production costs. Profits fell and soon it was discovered that soft toys could be made far more cheaply in the Far East which began to flood the market.

By 1968, when Wendy's health began to fail and the demand for soft toys had dropped, she decided to sell out to Denys Fisher Toys which continued to produce Wendy Boston soft toys until 1976 when it too was finally forced to close down.

*Left: A 1950s
Wendy Boston
bear filled with
foam chippings.*

"A Bear Called Paddington"

One Christmas, writer Michael Bond bought his wife a little brown bear. They decided to name him Paddington, after the London train station.

Bond wrote a story, *A Bear Called Paddington*, inspired by this little bear with his jar of marmalade and battered suitcase, and eventually went on to a total of 26 books. First published in 1958, Michael Bond's Paddington later had his own animated television programme. An English soft-toy company originally produced versions of Paddington and his Aunt Lucy who came to visit him from darkest Peru.

With his famous red wellington boots, Paddington quickly became a big star. But the story was not really written for children. At first, Bond was just writing for his own pleasure – until after about ten days he discovered that he had written an entire book. Within a few years Paddington's adventures were being read to millions of children not only in Britain and America but throughout the world.

Until 1981, Michael Bond wrote a book each year as well as television and film scripts for the regular five-minute episodes shown by BBC TV each evening. More recently Hanna-Barbera created an American animated cartoon series and even now, nearly half a century later, Paddington Bear has lost none of his original popularity – especially with the film world.

Right: Michael Bond's Paddington Bear by R. J. Wright.

Michael Bond set up his own merchandising company for hundreds of Paddington-related items and, although he no longer controls this, demand is still high. The first soft-toy version of Paddington was created in 1971, by Gabrielle Clarkson. Aunt Lucy joined him and until 1976 Clarkson held the world exclusive rights. Now she only supplies to Britain. In America, Eden Toys produces its own version of Paddington, which is softer than the original, and does not wear wellington boots.

*Left: Paddington
Bear by
Gabrielle.*

A New Age Begins

In 1969 the teddy bear experienced an unexpected renaissance when the bear collector Peter Bull published a book about his hobby. Suddenly old-fashioned teddy bears were desirable again. A market for adult collectors emerged. At the same time a new area of collecting was being created by bear artists who were making high-quality hand-crafted bears to traditional designs.

Right: Three bears inspired by the stories of Peter Bull.

These days there is a large range of new bears to choose from. The cheapest bears are imported – mass-produced for the world market in the Far East. In Britain, America and Europe, two ranges of bears are often made. One range – safe and machine-washable – is for children. The other is for the growing collectors' market. Teddy bears made for the collectors' ranges are usually limited editions which are numbered. Some of these are based on old designs. Steiff still makes replicas of a few of its original ranges which have become collector's items.

Left: Artist bears by Loris Hancock, an Australian bear artist.

Bears From Australia

It is hard to find out whether any Australian-made bears were ever exported, but we do know that imported bears were sold in Australia for many years. In the 20s firms were established in Melbourne – Joy Toys – and Perth – Fideston Toys – for the mass-production of teddy bears in Australia. By the 1970s these were joined by Barton Waugh, Berlex, Emil, Jakas, Lindee and Verna.

In the late 1960s and early 70s, import tariffs were lifted on imported toys. This affected Australian-made teddy bears badly. Almost all the Australian toymakers established from 1920 on simply could not compete with the flood of inexpensive Asian imports and went out of business. This was the catalyst for the birth of the Australian artist bear market– which has grown to become a flourishing sector today

*Right: A steiff
Original Teddy.*

Left: Steiff's baby bear – very rare and highly collectable.

The earliest Australian bears were of exceptionally high quality, beautifully designed and made from the finest imported English mohair. They featured glass eyes and were always uniquely Australian.

Joy Toys, established in Melbourne, Victoria, during the early 1920s, was an imaginative and energetic business which made gorgeous bears. Until the company was bought by Cyclops in the 1960s, it is estimated that they produced over 50,000 bears. Joy Toys made bears in many different styles.

Right: A very early Joy Toys bear dating back to 1925 with curved paws and clear glass eyes painted on the backs.

At first they were fully jointed and filled with excelsior. Their slim torsos and limbs were similar to early German bears. In the 1930s, the neck was no longer jointed and the traditional Joy Toy trademark appeared. From this time the design was more like the English-made bears – with the exception of their upturned paws.

Gradually the filling was changed to kapok and from the 1950s crumbed rubber was used for stuffing. But by the 1960s, the excellent quality had started to deteriorate and although the name Joy Toys is now owned by Toltoys it has not been used since 1976.

The Fideston Toy Company started its life as a book and music depot. Set up in Bunbury, Western Australia by Louisa and Richard Fiddes, during the First World War. Mrs Fiddes began making soft toys when it was impossible to obtain imported toys. Her products became so popular that she fulfilled her first teddy bear order in 1917 and was the very first commercial teddy bear maker in Australia.

A NEW AGE FOR BEARS

In 1921 the Fideston Toy Company was registered. A factory was established in a suburb of Perth and the mass production of soft toys for Australian children began. Fourteen family members were employed as the business expanded rapidly until by the 1930s they were producing a range of toys. Bears were easily the most popular and they were producing over 1,000 each month.

Emil Pty Ltd was set up to make soft toys and bears from about the middle of the 1930s. They had various factories in and around Melbourne, Victoria. The design was extremely handsome, with a broad head and wide-apart ears. The distinctive nose was sewn in black thread with two long outside stitches. As time went on the quality of the mohair used began to deteriorate but, although the bears were eventually no

longer fully jointed, glass eyes had been replaced by plastic and paw pads were made of white vinyl, the shape of the nose always remained the same. By the 1970s, they were no longer able to compete with the cheaper Asian imports and ceased trading.

Any old Australian bears which have survived and can be found today are highly prized by collectors because of their unique Australian features. They can usually be identified by their labels, the characteristic upturned paws, and serious expression on the face.

One of the earliest and rarest Australian teddy bears is a teddy-koala which was made about 1910. He must have originally had a fur coat, but wear and tear over the years has left him with a very strange leather look.

Left: Modern Artist bears. The larger bear is by Kathy Harry an Australian Bear Artist and the small bear is by Junko Tanaka, a Japanese bear artist.

TREASURE TROVE COLLECTING

There was an Old Person of Ware,

Who rode on the back of a bear,

When ask'd 'Does it trot?'

He said, 'Certainly not!

He's a Moppsikon, Floppiskon Bear!'

Edward Lear

Right: Two 1950s English bears.

Two or three decades ago who would have imagined that their old childhood teddy bear might be highly sought after as a collector's item? Given to jumble sales or just thrown out, countless teddy bears simply disappeared in the 40s, 50s and 60s.

From about the 1970s, however, gradually people began to take an interest in their old bears. In London specialist toy fairs began to be held and the opportunity to find and collect old toys – including dolls and bears – became very popular. The plaintive stare of a one-eyed threadbare teddy began to charm people who had perhaps lost their own precious childhood teddy bear and jumped at the chance to buy a replacement.

Car boot sales and jumble sales became favourite hunting grounds for treasure-trove teddies. Collectors bought everything they could find – and still wanted more. A second wave of teddy bear fever had begun.

Teddy bear mania hit the news. Fetching amazingly high prices, teddy bears began to appear at London auctions and soon people were ransacking their attics in the hope of discovering some long-forgotten, dusty once-treasured teddy bear.

*Left: A rare
coloured Yes/No
bear by Schuco.*

Now, 30 years on, that particular expression on the face of an old teddy bear can turn you into an obsessed teddy bear collector. Once bitten by the bug, there is no escape. And you will certainly not be alone. Some people will only collect bears made by famous manufacturers. Others find that the greatest appeal lies in well loved and well worn bears with no pedigree.

Right: A 1925 Bing bear.

Even for serious collectors, financial gain is rarely the sole motivation. All over the world there are now hundreds of thousands of collectors trying to recapture part of their childhood – and enjoying one of the most rewarding obsessions imaginable.

Right: A pair of 1920s Chad Valley bears.

Exactly how people collect bears is a matter of personal taste. Because, since their introduction, teddies have been cuddled and played with like dolls, the two are closely connected in collectors' minds. Many makers made both dolls and teddy bears, and specialist sales frequently contain both dolls and bears.

TREASURE TROVE COLLECTING

What to Look For

Who collects bears? A childhood present of a teddy bear or perhaps a bear handed down from a relative often inspires a collector. For a long time bears have been associated with the little romantic gifts given to loved ones for anniversaries and birthdays. This is enough to spark off a collector.

Whilst some people will only collect new bears made by a teddy bear artist or one of the famous manufacturers such as Steiff and Gebrüder Hermann in Germany or Dean's and Merrythought in England, others will only collect bears from a certain period – such as before the Second World War.

Bears from around the world vary in every possible way. It is possible to find a teddy bear wherever you live or travel to. In some countries collectors can find bears to buy quite easily; others have to travel widely to add to their collection. A bear hunt is a matter of personal taste because collectors have such varied interests.

Left: These bears are of unknown makers and date back to 1912.

For those who collect bears by colour, black bears seem to be the most popular. Whilst this limits choice, it also presents a challenge. Coloured bears look most attractive when they are displayed together and provide a wide variety. During the 1920s and 1930s, coloured bears were produced in various colours – blue, green, white, purple, lilac, orange and pink.

Right: These two delightful Steiffs are dressed in period clothing and date back to 1908.

There are collectors who will only buy vintage bears which are in perfect condition, unrestored and fully documented by named makers complete with their labels. Others look for battered bears with their own well worn charm. These can be found, made by unidentified makers, often for lower prices and become a great asset to an interesting and varied collection.

Modern dressed bears can be found made by artists; vintage bears may often wear delightful period clothes with interesting stories and sometimes are even accompanied by photographs of their original owner and a family history.

Unusual bears include red, white and blue miniature mascot bears from the First World War; a multi-coloured Chiltern Hugmee bear from the 1930s; a German musical bear dating from the 1920s; and twin bears from about 1910 dressed in old christening robes. One of the many bears on the market in the 1930s was dressed as a clown; a 1920s mechanical Schuco bear appeared fully dressed in scarlet military uniform; and the gorgeous Teddy Rose was made in 1925 by Steiff and is available as a replica in a limited edition of 10,000 made in 1987. The House of Nisbet produced a replica of Aloysius the *Brideshead Revisited* bear in 1987 whilst Gund made a delightful synthetic plush panda in the 1940s.

TREASURE TROVE COLLECTING

Miniature bears are extremely popular with some collectors. Schuco, the German manufacturer, made a large range of miniature bears in the 1920s and many of these were in unusually bright colours. Some collectors love to have the bright cheerful miniature bears in their collection, where they complement the bears made by Steiff which are still in great demand. There are lots of charming miniature bears which do not come from any well known maker and these can be irresistible.

In the early days of motoring, cars sometimes had teddy bear mascots on their bonnets, and these can still be found in some quite unlikely places. Although they are sought after today, car boot sales often prove a treasure trove for serious collectors who know what they are looking for.

In the early 20th century there was quite a craze for novelty bears and manufacturers catered for this demand. Some highly original and ingenious products disguised as simple toys were produced, revealing their true purpose when a body was opened or a head was unscrewed. Novelties such as a dice holder and a Schuco perfume bear are rare and collectors prize them highly.

Left: Miniature bears are highly collectable. Schuco made a variety of charming miniatures including perfume bottle bears (above left) and other novelties (below left) including small mechanical bears on wheels.

TREASURE TROVE COLLECTING

Bear collecting is not all about making a profit. As with many antique collectors, the real purpose is simply for the enjoyment. Lovely old bears with their slightly shabby mellow charm are just as attractive as the delightful bright faces of jaunty new bears. To a true bear lover, happiness is just bear-shaped.

These are the guidelines you should take care to follow once you have done some essential background reading on the fascinating subject of teddy bear collecting:

What is the bear's condition?

What does the bear look like?

Does the bear have a label?

Is the bear jointed?

What fabric has been used?

What position are the ears in?

What are the eyes made of?

What type of nose does the bear have?

What are the paw pads made from?

What has the bear been stuffed with?

Right: A 1950s Chiltern bear.

If you decide to begin a bear collection you can easily run out of space and you may decide to go only for the bargain bears to be found at jumble sales and markets. If you go on to become a serious bear collector, it is useful to have a checklist and, if possible, a good book which contains a price guide to help you spend your money wisely.

TREASURE TROVE COLLECTING

Bear collecting is now such a popular pastime that there are a lot of fake bears on the market and you could be very disappointed if you have paid a lot of money for a bear which does not turn out to be what you thought you were buying.

It has been known for fake bears to be deliberately produced to deceive unwary buyers, who can also be confused between new artist bears or replica bears with labels on. Although the latter are based on the traditional designs by famous makers, they must not be confused with an original old teddy bear with a genuine history.

Left: A 1910 American bear.

Armed with some knowledge you can avoid the heartbreak of losing money – however much you may love the bear you have chosen.

CHECKLIST:

1. Examine the bear very carefully to make sure that no damage has been concealed. Look under any clothes if the bear is dressed in case there are threadbare patches or a limb has been cunningly replaced. It is difficult – although not impossible – to replace thin rotting material and you need to be sure of what you are taking on.

Left: The distinctive hump-back shape of an early Steiff.

Far left: Chiltern and Stieff labels.

2. If the bear's arms and muzzle are longer than normal and if it has a hump, it can mean that the bear was made in the very early days of the 20th century. This could be a vintage bear. Generally speaking, bears made after the Second World War will almost certainly have flatter faces and much shorter arms. Try to find out all you can about the different manufacturers because this will often give you a clue as to their distinctive shapes.

3. The best way to identify your bear is if it has a label. However, many of the earlier bears that originally had rather flimsy tags for labels have lost them. Embroidered labels and metal tags can sometimes be found attached to older bears.

Left: Two unjointed Chiltern bears dating from the 1960s.

4. Many of the older bears have invisible round cardboard joints. By the 1960s, however, some bears were actually made unjointed. French and Japanese manufacturers preferred external joints. Australian bears almost always had unjointed necks.

5. Wool mohair would have been used for real vintage bears. From around 1930, artificial silk plush was used. Other fabrics in synthetic materials such as nylon plush were used from the 1950s on. French bears were often made from cotton plush or short mohair. The appearance and texture of these different fabrics are quite distinctive and it is a good idea to study them and become familiar with the way they actually feel.

6. Look carefully at the bear's ears. You can check them against similar old bears in pictures or advertisements to see what position they are in. Check carefully for any holes in the head seams where any original ears might have once been to make sure that the ears are not replacements.

Right: A 1908 Steiff bear in superb condition, with black button eyes and cardboard disc joints held together with metal pinnings.

7. The eyes of any bear made before the beginning of the First World War should have been boot buttons. From the early 1920s glass was more commonly used by all manufacturers although some British bears from slightly earlier may be found with glass eyes. From the 1950s you should expect to find plastic eyes.

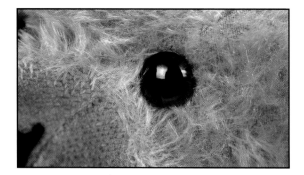

8. Look carefully at the nose stitching. This is most important because each manufacturer had its own distinctive nose stitching. Sometimes noses have been replaced with black wool and this is definitely incorrect. Noses were generally woven from silk thread. In the 1950s and 1960s, the use of rubber noses became common.

10. The weight of the bear will give you an important clue about the stuffing. A light older bear will have kapok stuffing. An English-made bear will have had some wood wool added. Where the stuffing is entirely of wood wool the bear will have a crunchy feel. After 1940 a bear may have sub stuffing. Later bears were stuffed with lightweight foam. French bears were made with excelsior far later than in England and Germany. Most of the early French bears were hard-stuffed.

9. Have the paw pads been replaced? For vintage bears, the most common material used for paw pads was felt. In Australia cotton was often used and because this does not wear well any pads will almost certainly have been replaced. By the 1930s, velveteen and rexine were very popular for paw pads. Some later bears may have pads of plush, leather or suede.

Left: The weight of a bear will give you a clue about the stuffing. This smart 1920s Bing is stuffed with wood wool.

Buying Old Teddy Bears

If you are a new collector buying from a dealer, you must always make sure that your source is reputable. Ask for a receipt which details the description of your purchase and names the maker with a statement of the age of the bear.

When buying from a fair, you should keep a record of the dealer's address in case you should need to contact him again at some future date. If you buy from an auction, you must retain the catalogue description as a record of your purchase and remember to examine the teddy bear very carefully when taking possession of it. Since you first viewed it, it may have been damaged and a bear which you have taken home and discovered to be flawed will not always be returnable.

Even though you may be delighted and gratified to see the value of your collection grow, this should really not be the sole motive of your hobby. All prices can fluctuate – down as well as up – and your most important consideration should always be that you really like your bear.

Right: A 1930s Chiltern Hugmee bear.

TREASURE TROVE COLLECTING

Social History

The appeal of collecting is universal and elementary. Antique teddy bears provide delicious insights into the lives of children of the past – they were always objects of great affection. The fascinating social history provided by old teddy bears reflects the many dramatic social changes which took place throughout the 20th century.

Increased media interest in old teddy bears fuelled the upsurge in their popularity as collector's items and now you are most unlikely to find a genuine original Steiff teddy bear in a car boot sale.

But it is still possible to find old teddy bears at a wide range of prices so, no matter how limited your budget, there is always something for every collector. For a new collector it is vital to handle and examine as many teddy bears as possible before spending money on your first purchase – which may well be costly. Read around the subject and visit auction houses when there is a specialist teddy bear sale where they are laid out for viewing and it is easy for you to examine them and learn about their characteristics.

Left: This very rare dual-coloured dolly bear is a Steiff and dates back to 1912.

Auctions and Fairs

A wide range of teddy bears is often included in specialist auctions and the catalogue should identify the maker and age of a bear with an estimated value. It will not always mention damage, however, and you need to have sharp eyes. It is absolutely crucial to examine a bear thoroughly and take into account the cost of any restoration which might be necessary. Remember, once you have bought a teddy bear at auction, if you later discover even the smallest amount of damage, it probably cannot be returned. So scrutinise each bear very thoroughly.

Specialist teddy bear fairs are another opportunity for you to see large numbers of antique bears. Many are held in London and may be attended by dealers from the United States and many European countries. They will include many examples of teddy bears and dealers will usually be only too happy to provide information about their bears and advise you.

at auction, more people have started to search their homes for old teddy bears and the result is that more bears than ever before are appearing on the market.

For many of us, teddy bear collecting begins by accident. A present of a bear, or maybe the inheritance of a treasured family teddy from a relation, or perhaps the decision to buy a new bear to keep a childhood bear company, suddenly begins a collection.

If you want to start a serious collection of bears that you hope will appreciate in value, then there are several factors to take into consideration.

Starting Your Collection

Right: These two 1930s Steiff bears are both made in unusual mohair colours.

It can be a bewildering experience for the beginner to decide what to collect. The choice is huge. In the last few years manufacturers and bear artists have joined the stampede to fulfil the demand for new teddy bears. Because old bears are now fetching enormous prices

TREASURE TROVE COLLECTING

What to Collect

Old bears, in common with any antiques, will be most desirable if they are in perfect condition. But of course these will be the hardest to find and the most expensive.

For an inexperienced collector it is a good idea to start off by going to a reputable dealer who will be able to explain the characteristics of the different makers to you. This is important because many of the oldest bears no longer have their original identifying labels. A good dealer will always give you proper help, advice – and most importantly – a genuine receipt for any purchase.

If you decide to collect bears made by well known manufacturers, you should became as familiar as you can with their identifying characteristics. This book provides a short guide which will give you the basic information you will need about some of the different labels and buttons used by various manufacturers.

Keep your eyes open for forgeries. Flea markets are usually the places for these. Old, tatty bears placed artfully in the middle of a pile of bric-a-brac can look like the genuine article.

Perhaps the very nicest collections are those which have a few bears in perfect condition living with others who have suffered from obvious wear and tear throughout their lives. After all, bears are toys. And most toys, especially teddy bears, have had to put up with a great deal over their lives as a child's treasured companion. Often they have had the stuffing knocked out of them by too much loving attention and their fur has become threadbare in places through constant cuddling.

Left: This mint condition Chad Valley bear dates back to 1938 and would be a great find for a collector because of his condition.

Left: This beautiful Schuco Yes/No bear is complete with her original clothes from the 1950s.

Repairs

If you wonder about repairing an old teddy bear, don't be fooled into thinking that this may adversely affect its value. Provided the work is undertaken sensitively, using the most appropriate material, this will help the bear to live much longer and sometimes it can even add to its value. Restoring bears definitely conserves them – and if a bear is left neglected, with its stuffing spilling out, his fur dirty and uncared-for, it will never gain in value.

Right: A great deal can be done to repair an old bear provided the original fabric is strong enough and there is plenty of fur left.

A great deal can be done to repair an old bear provided the original fabric is strong enough and there is plenty of fur left. Of course, a very bald bear can be given very little help because weakened fabric will not hold any stitches well enough to sustain a repair job. Don't try to repair a teddy bear if the fabric feels thin or hard and is crisp or brittle to the touch. If it is full of holes and is splitting very little can be done. It is often hard to replace missing limbs and ears because matching the original mohair exactly will be impossible.

But many battered bears have great appeal. If you do decide to restore your bear, remember that if it can be cleaned and mended it can retain its original endearing characteristics – twisted nose, odd eyes or lopsided ears. Stuffing can be replaced, pads can be replaced or repaired, eyes replaced and nose restitched – and, gently handled, it can look very handsome again.

Identification

Do ask about a bear's history if you are fortunate enough to buy a bear from its original owner or their family. Perhaps you can discover where and when it was bought, whether there are any interesting stories associated with it – and, most importantly, its name. Sometimes you may also acquire a photograph of it with its original owner and these records are all well worth preserving because they will add to a bear's value considerably.

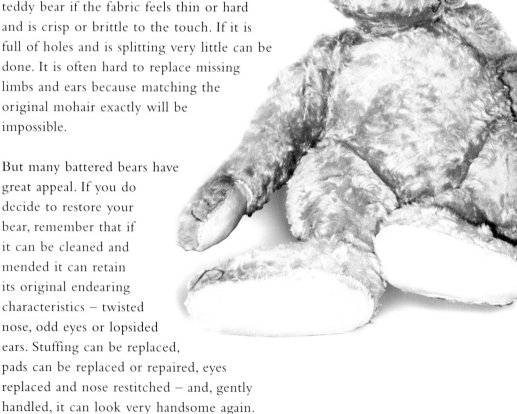

New Bears

A very popular area of bear collecting, which is growing all the time, is for artist bears. Around the world there are now hundreds of artist bear-makers who design and hand-make their own bears. Many artist bear-makers are very popular with waiting lists for their bears which may run to a year or even more. At fairs, some of the best-known artist bear-makers will have sold their entire stock within the first hour.

Imported mass-produced bears from the Far East are the cheapest in a large range of new bears currently available. In Britain, America and Europe manufacturers often make two ranges – a safe machine-washable design for children and a collectors' range which is usually based on old patterns and produced in limited numbered editions. Steiff still makes replicas of some of its original designs which have become collector's items in their own right.

Price

A very important consideration when starting a collection is how much you will be prepared to spend on any one bear. You will then know from the beginning that you are aiming, say, to assemble a limited collection of very early genuine bears and you will buy very carefully. You will realise that the better the condition of the bear and the older it is, the more expensive it is likely to be. And you will be on the lookout for fakes.

That is not to say that you won't stumble over a bargain at a jumble sale or market. And there is always the possibility that a bear you bought just because you loved it turns out to be valuable because it is rare.

Size

Any sensible collector will consider very early on the amount of space available for display. The amount of space bears can take up is surprising and this may influence your decision about buying too many large bears. A variety of sizes can be very attractive and, if space is an issue, you can still build up a good collection of smaller or miniature bears.

Left: An English modern artist's bear, from "Bears that are Special" by Pam Howells.

A GUIDE TO EARLY MANUFACTURERS

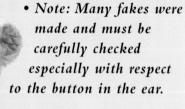

Teddy, Teddy, You're my sweetheart true

You're never bold,

You never scold,

You all my troubles share.

What would I do without you dear,

Old Teddy Teddy Bear

Traditional

A Quick Guide to Early Bears

STEIFF

Check:
- **Is the bear made from mohair plush?**
- **Are eyes made from boot button or glass?**
- **Is it filled with excelsior or kapok stuffing?**
- **Is the snout realistic in shape and prominently pointed?**
- **Are eyes set relatively close together just above the muzzle?**
- **Is the nose stitched in brown or black thread?**
- **Does the bear have a pronounced hump at the top of the back?**
- **Are the arms long and curved?**
- **Are the legs long with narrow ankles, large oval feet and felt paw pads?**
- **If the bear is made from blond, white gold or brown mohair, does it have four or five stitched claws?**
- **Is the bear tagged with a button in the ear?**

Further check:
As bears became more popular throughout the early 20th century some changes appeared in Steiff bears:

- **Snouts became shorter and flatter**
- **Humps became smaller and less pronounced**
- **Claws may have been omitted.**
- **Cheaper black short mohair plush may have been used.**
- **Unusual colours may have been used**
  - **Note: Many fakes were made and must be carefully checked especially with respect to the button in the ear.**

Right: "Tubby" a beautiful 1910 Steiff bear with black boot-button eyes.

Left: Two novelty bears with muzzles dating from 1910. These bears were inspired by the dancing bears which were a popular form of entertainment all over Europe around this time.

CHAD VALLEY

Right: A 1925 Chad Valley bear.

Check:
- *Is the filling made of a mixture of kapok and excelsior?*
- *Is the body fat with chubby or short limbs?*
- *Does the bear have a wide head?*
- *Is the snout long, blunt and/or clipped?*
- *Are the ears large and flat?*
- *Does the bear have amber and black glass eyes attached by wires?*
- *Is the nose bulbous and heavily stitched?*
- *Are feet relatively small?*
- *Is the bear marked or labelled?*

Right: A 1925 Chad Valley bear with a manufacturer's button under his chin.

MERRYTHOUGHT LTD PRE-1940S

Check:

• Is the body made from mohair plush and jointed?

• Is the stuffing a mixture of kapok and excelsior?

• Are the ears widely spaced?

• Is the muzzle clipped and pointed in shape?

• Are the eyes well rounded, set low in the head and made of glass?

• Is the nose rectangular in shape and embroidered with vertical stitches?

• Does the bear have embroidered claws on the paws with a connecting link stitch?

• Are the feet quite small with felt, cotton or velveteen pads?

• Is the bear marked with a label on the foot or a button in the back or ear?

Left: A Merrythought label stitched to the base of a bear's foot.

Left: These Mr and Mrs Twisty Cheeky bears date from 1966. They were made by Merrythought and had an internal wire frame to allow them to be bent into different positions.

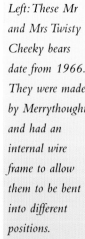
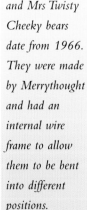

Right: These two 1930s Chad Valley bears display the beautiful yellow and black eyes typical of Chad bears at this time as well as their wide, thickly stitched noses.

Left: This 1950s Chiltern Hugmee bear has an unshaved muzzle, characteristic of the period. He has long tapered arms with velvet paw and foot pads.

CHILTERN

Right: A typical Chiltern bear from the 1930s with a wide head and large ears.

Check:

• **Does the bear have a wide head and large ears?**

• **If the nose is stitched, are there upward stitches at each end?**

• **Are the eyes made from glass?**

• **Is the body filled with kapok or excelsior?**

• **Does the bear have long curving arms?**

• **If the bear has wide feet, are they reinforced with card?**

• **Is the bear made from soft high-quality mohair?**

• **Is it marked with a label on a foot?**

Right: Two 1950s Chiltern Hugmee bears.

IDEAL NOVELTY & TOY CO.

Check:

- **Is the bear made from short mohair?**
- **Is the stuffing made from a mixture of kapok and excelsior?**
- **Is the head triangular-shaped with a shorn muzzle and fabric or stitched nose?**
- **Are the eyes made from boot buttons or glass?**
- **Are the ears large and situated on the side of the head?**
- **Is the snout prominently angled?**
- **Is the mouth stitched?**
- **Is the body jointed with barrel-shaped or humped torso?**
- **Are the pads pointed at the tips?**

Left: An early American Ideal bear of 1910.

ARTIST AND OTHER NEW BEARS

It's a very funny thought that if bears were bees,

They'd build their nests at the bottom of trees.

A. A. Milne

With the move away from the traditional bears of the beginning of the 20th century towards more mass-produced designs, the first artist bears began to appear on the west coast of America in the 1980s. Before long other countries followed suit and now teddy bear artistry is a big business.

Countries as far afield as Japan, New Zealand, the Netherlands, France, Austria and Switzerland are well known for their beautiful and original artist bears. These attract many collectors who are prepared to travel long distances on their own personal bear hunt.

By 1980, Steiff had introduced modern copies of some of their traditional bears in limited editions – the first ever teddy bear replicas had reached the market.

Most of the surviving long-established factories – which include Dean's and Merrythought in Britain, Steiff and Gebrüder Hermann in Germany and Thiennot in France – now make replica bears for the collectors' market. Special limited and anniversary editions are made which are specifically aimed at collectors. Dean's and Steiff have formed their own collectors' clubs.

Increasing competition from the Far East caused many of the early teddy bear manufacturers to discontinue trading. In Australia almost all the factories had ceased production by the end of the 1970s. In France the story was the same, and in Britain many of the famous manufacturers were bought out by larger companies, whose business was to import cheaper toys from the Far East.

Right: An English artist bear by Elaine Lonsdale.

ARTIST AND OTHER NEW BEARS

The few survivors included the familiar names of Dean's in England, Ideal in America and Steiff in Germany and they managed to continue to produce high-quality teddy bears. They recaptured the traditional elements of their early toys and now, more than two decades on, these are highly collectible in their own right. At the same time, many teddy bears had become famous characters, made immensely popular by children's television programmes which provided a wonderful opportunity to launch soft-toy versions. Rupert Bear, Winnie the Pooh and Paddington Bear were all made during this period

Bear Artists

Bear artists design and make their own distinctive bears, often with the help of family, friends and out-workers for all but the unique finishing touches. These artists have very creative imaginations as well as the excellent technical skills required to make a teddy bear correctly.

Artist bears are usually produced in small limited editions which make them very collectible in their own right. They can be bought directly from the artist by mail order, at bear fairs worldwide and at teddy bear shops.

Australia

Among the top bear artists in Australia, Heather Brooks, Lexie Haworth, Rosalie Maclennan, Briony Nottage and Deborah Sargentson are famous for producing outstanding bears which are both traditional and experimental, using a wide variety of materials. Normally they appear as one of a kind or in very limited editions.

Left: An Australian "Rainforest Bear" by Loris Hancock.

ARTIST AND OTHER NEW BEARS

America

Well known bear artists in America include Gloria Franks, Elaine Fujita-Gamble, Frances Harper, Mary Holdstadt, Susan Horn and Kathleen Wallace. Various designs and materials are used for these individual bears, combined with fine workmanship and a great attention to detail which mean that many of them have won awards and featured in teddy bear magazines worldwide.

Right: An English black artist bear made by Lyne Bèrube.

Canada

Hana Franklin, Cherie Friendship, Lesley Mallet and Joan Rankin are among the top bear artists in Canada who create character bears, write stories, make, collect and sell bears worldwide.

England

In England, Penny Chalmers, Jo Greeno, Gregory Gyllenship, Stacey Lee Terry, Nicola Perkins, Jennie Sharman-Cox and Frank Wallace make many different-sized dressed, cartoon and character bears using mainly traditional materials.

ARTIST AND OTHER NEW BEARS

Other Countries

Bear artists in other countries include Joan Hanna in Ireland, Aline Cousin, Marylou Jouet and Marcelle Goffin in France, Jean Van Meeuwe Slater in Belgium, Jane Humme and Annemieke Koetse in the Netherlands, Karin Koller in Switzerland, Karin Kronsteiner in Austria, Heidrun Winkler, Ineke, Vera and Verena in Germany and Mary Kelly in South Africa. In New Zealand Cimarron Lang, Janis Harris and Frances McCleary produce replica and award-winning bears, while in Japan Michi Takahashi, Miyuki Wada and Mayumi Watanabe design, make and sell their own distinctive teddy bears for a world market.

Bear Manufacturers Today

There are various categories of manufactured teddy bears on the market today. The old makers like Steiff and Merrythought produce limited-edition replicas of their original designs in addition to completely new bear designs, sometimes actually employing famous bear artists. These artists will design new limited-edition bears, which means that collectors can acquire high-quality well designed teddy bears at reasonable prices.

In order to meet the continuing huge demand in Europe and America, many new manufacturers have emerged. Some of these operate in the Far East where labour is cheap so that collectors can afford the excellent quality and design on offer.

*Left:
'Something's Bruin' by top British artist Jill Baxter.*

*Right: American
artist, Joan
Woessner's bear
sits alongside an
old Nette bear.*

Being able to produce two ranges of teddy
bears is cost-effective and ensures that teddy
bears are still being produced as children's
toys as well as satisfying the growing
collectors' market.

CLEMENS

Clemens, whose first bears were made from
blankets which were left over from the
Second World War, now make bears by hand
to the very highest standards using the finest
materials. Among their recent bears is a
replica of a bear originally produced in 1962
and a Millennium bear.

DEAN'S

Dean's have introduced a new Elite range to
make use of the huge variety of unusual
mohair materials available today. A limited
edition designed by Jill Baxter for their
Artist Showcase Range in 1991 has proved
very prestigious and sought after.

ARTIST AND OTHER NEW BEARS

GUND

Gund, as one of America's oldest soft-toy companies, produces new collections as small limited editions, as well as an exclusive one-of-a-kind luxury teddy bear which comes packaged and bearing the award-winning graphics which were originally on the Gund bears from the 1930s.

Left: A new collectable bear manufactured by the American company Gund.

ARTIST AND OTHER NEW BEARS

GEBRÜDER HERMANN

Gebrüder Hermann, the famous German manufacturer from the early 1900s, produces each bear with its distinctive red Hermann Original Teddy badge. Thousands of these bears are still being made by skilled workers using fine-quality handmade fabrics for the world market. An unusual new design, made of string mohair, was recently made as a limited edition of 2,000.

MERRYTHOUGHT

Merrythought acquired the rights to use the name Alpha Farnell in 1996 and produced a replica of a 1930s Farnell bear which was copied exactly from the original and made in a limited edition of 250. To commemorate the start of the 21st century a bear was designed exclusively for the company, wearing an embellished silver button bearing a Birmingham hallmark and issued in a limited edition of only 1,000.

THE NORTH-AMERICAN BEAR COMPANY INC.

The North-American Bear Company Inc., founded in 1978, is now an immensely successful name in the teddy bear world producing a Classic range of bears as well as their famous Muffy – a member of the Vanderbear family.

RUSS BERRIE AND CO.

Russ Berrie and Co. were founded in the early 1970s and are now the largest toy-distributing company in the world. Two of their collections include Bears from the Past and the Vintage Mohair Collection – many of their bears are well known worldwide for their irresistible "impulse gift" appeal.

STEIFF

Steiff, as the original and most famous name for teddy bears, have brought out a replica of the hugely popular 1928 Petsy Bear, and as an exclusive for Harrods a Centenary Bear in a limited edition of 2,000.

Caring for Bears

Both newly purchased teddy bears and bears that have been cleaned and restored must be carefully looked after. A little regular maintenance will keep them looking fresh and attractive.

Do not sit your bears in direct light – for instance on a windowsill as this will dry them out and they will both fade and rot. All bears should have a cool place where they can sit, out of direct sunlight. Don't be tempted to keep your bears in polythene bags in the mistaken belief that this will help to preserve them. If your bears are not going to be displayed, then they should be carefully wrapped in an old cotton pillow-slip or acid-free tissue paper before being placed in a cardboard box and stored in a cool, dry place.

It is a priority to keep your bears as dust-free as possible. Regular grooming using a soft brush together with an annual wipe-down, using a damp cloth which has been soaked in warm water and wrung out, should be undertaken.

In order to deter moths, which will seriously
damage your bears, place lavender bags and
cedar blocks nearby.

Handle all your bears gently,
especially the old ones. Once
they are no longer
needed to fulfil their
role as children's
toys and they are
retired, they should
be treated with the
respect they have earned.

*Left: Top
German artist
Marie
Robeshon's bear
'Robin-de-Bär'.*

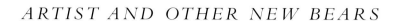

Display

It is entirely your own choice when you begin to think about displaying your collection of bears. No doubt you will have already considered the amount of space you have available and the size of the bears in your collection. Perhaps you will decide to put up some shelves in a spare room for them, or you may want to display them in your living room so that they are still part of everyday family life.

Do make sure that wherever you display your precious bears they are out of harm's way. Children and animals can be a hazard and your fragile older bears will not stand up to rough or careless handling. Even displaying an old bear on a bed where it will require constant handling – albeit carefully – is not a good idea because damage will inevitably occur.

Right: Two 1910 Steiff bears.

Dressing your bears may be an extra challenge which you wish to undertake. Although some people prefer to leave their bears exactly as they found them, for some bears it is a practical advantage to wear clothes which will protect fragile fur and stuffing.

ARTIST AND OTHER NEW BEARS

If you know that your home will visited by children and animals from time to time, perhaps you should consider special shelving which is out of reach – or, alternatively, use glass-fronted cabinets for extra protection.

If you do decide to dress some of your bears, remember to try and find something from the period when the bear was made. If you have a vintage bear, it will look its best wearing vintage clothes and it is well worth while spending a little time and effort locating something suitable. Antique fairs can sometimes be a good source of clothing.

Perhaps your bear has come to you already dressed. Some bears wear the clothes that were originally made for them by their first owners and, of course, you will want to leave these clothes in place. Maybe you are lucky enough to have a photograph of an original owner and this can always add to your display.

Modern artist bears often come undressed and you may decide to make your own clothes for them. Knitted or crocheted clothes are easy to make and can look very attractive. If you can't make your own, there are various stalls at markets which sell clothes and accessories for teddy bears which you can buy. Prices are usually quite reasonable and you will have fun experimenting with unusual ways of dressing your own bears.

Left: When you begin to think about displaying your bears you need to consider the amount of space you need for your collection – whether you have three or 30 bears.

Beware of Fakes

If you spend some time familiarising yourself with the characteristics of different bears and the fabrics used to make them, you will be less likely to be taken in by a fake.

Steiff is a popular choice for bear counterfeiters and several small points may help you to avoid an expensive mistake. Often the feet of a Steiff fake will be long, like the original, but not quite the right shape – perhaps with pads of cotton or leather which were never used by Steiff on their genuine vintage bears.

Sometimes fakes will actually turn up at auction houses – although flea markets and antique shows tend to be the favourite places for those who want to pass off a fake bear as original. With the rise of internet trading it is essential not to rely on simply a photograph of what is described as a genuine vintage bear – always see a bear face to face before parting with your money.

The best safeguard against fraud is to equip yourself with as much information as you can, buy from a reputable source and always make sure you get a proper headed receipt which is detailed and dated.

And remember that boot fairs and flea markets can still turn up an unexpected authentic bargain bear.

Right: a beautiful 1918 Farnell bear.

Left: A group of 1950s Schuco pandas.

DESIGNER BEARS

If I were a bear,

And a big bear too,

I shouldn't much care

If it froze or snew

I shouldn't much mind

If it snowed or friz —

I'd be all fur-lined

With a coat like his!

From Now We are Six
A.A. Milne

Although bears had been used as images for design long before the creation of the stuffed teddy bear in 1903 it was the teddy bear which truly caught the imagination of the public. The teddy bear was used by many different manufacturers to promote their products – and these varied from brandy to sweets and chocolates and from cereals to clothing.

Over the years the shape of bears in design has changed to reflect changing consumer tastes. A fascinating statement of social history throughout the 20th century can be traced through the advertisements, postcards, music, greetings cards, toys, games and ornaments which were produced using the image of the bear.

Humour was one of the most obvious subjects for the bear to illustrate, particularly where it was drawn in a realistically human pose, full of obvious mischief. Cuddly, jolly and often naughty, the earliest bears in advertisements caught the imagination of the public especially where the drawings were of real bears rather than teddy bears.

Teddy bear collectors need not be limited to stuffed toy bears – there is a variety of bear memorabilia made during the 19th century before the appearance of the teddy bear.

The great popularity of performing bears led to their images appearing on pottery, china and silver bought for and used in the home. In the early 20th century carved wooden bears which were known as Black Forest Bears were produced as desk ornaments and accessories for smokers. The appearance of the teddy bear led to items made for babies such as teething rings and rattles.

DESIGNER BEARS

*Left: A 1920s
dual-coloured
mohair Jopi bear.*

Right: These two
Schuco Yes/No
bears have
movements
activated by the
tails.

Left: This 1950s Yes/No bear has the Tricky label of Schuco. The design of these bears had changed dramatically from the pre-World War II bears, especially in the arms with their broad down-turned paws, their pronounced shaven muzzle and wide set eyes. This bear is also musical.

DESIGNER BEARS

Fashion accessories – silver earrings, hatpins and brooches – were popular gifts. Gold and silver pendants, bracelets and rings were and still are made. And throughout the century children's china – baby mugs and dishes and dolls' teasets – were decorated with delightful bears in various designs. Today these are highly collectible items.

Flea markets and boot fairs are excellent sources to find all sorts of bear memorabilia in a wide price range. The earliest bear pieces will fetch high prices today, but some of the newer pieces can be bought for quite reasonable prices as bear decoration is still popular.

Among the bear memorabilia to look out for are a Black Forest bear bell made in about 1900, a Black Forest cuckoo clock made in carved wood, a Black Forest inkwell and pen made in about 1912, Swiss bear brushes and cork stoppers, tobacco jars and inkwells.

Coloured Bears

The popularity of coloured bears has grown steadily since they were first introduced before the First World War. The coloured bears which Steiff made in the very early years were not a great success because most people preferred to buy natural-looking bears in traditional colours.

A very few of the earliest Steiff coloured bears have in fact survived and, together with the later bears made by Cramer, Jopi and Schuco between the wars, these now command high prices.

The enormous boost to British companies due to the ban on German imports during the First World War led to the development of many new ideas. The use of alternative fabrics, especially art silk, synthetic plush and coloured mohair, led to the appearance of many coloured and novelty bears.

Chad Valley made blue, red, pink and rainbow-coloured bears – some examples of which still survive. Merrythought made a wide range of coloured bears in the 1930s and Dean's clown bear was in production as late as the 1950s.

DESIGNER BEARS

Miniature Bears

The most famous miniature toy teddy bears were made by Schuco between the 1920s and the 1970s and, of course, these are today highly collectible items. The range was extremely wide and included dressing-table and handbag novelties which were popular as gifts. Some bears were made with concealed perfume bottles and powder compacts, miniature dice and manicure sets.

In spite of their size, the miniature bears share the same high quality and attention to detail that the larger bears are made with and resemble them closely in style. One of the features of miniature teddy bears is that none of them have paw pads – apart from those which were made during the 1920s.

Schuco made their miniature bears in various colours which included, cream, red and gold. It is interesting to compare the different generations of miniature bears and how designs changed with the times.

Left: A selection of colourful miniature Schuco bears from the 1920s.

During the 1930s, Schuco produced a range of clockwork acrobatic bears, and small cars, called Rollers, were made for the tiny bears to ride in. The little cars were made of metal with three wheels, friction driven, in a variety of colours which are very sought after by today's collectors.

Musical Bears

Some long-haired, brightly coloured early musical bears contain squeeze-operated musical boxes and are thought to have been made by Jopi, although it is hard to date them exactly.

Japanese Bears

Right: A rare brightly coloured musical bear by Jopi, dating back to 1920.

Many of the designs used for Japanese bears were similar to early French and American teddy bears. Often they were made of very poor-quality materials – blanket wool or short bristle mohair instead of mohair plush. The shape of the bodies and limbs was long and narrow, with small round feet and pinched ears. Stuffing was usually excelsior and, although some bears were jointed, their joints were of poor quality with visible cardboard discs and wire rather than metal used to make the joints.

Only a few vintage bears were made in Japan and the Second World War resulted in most of these being destroyed. After the war, however, the business of making inexpensive teddy bears in Japan began to flourish. There was a huge market for cheaper toys in Europe and the United States and from about 1950 the Japanese began to make mechanical toys of all sorts – teddy bears with mechanical devices inside them were especially popular.

DESIGNER BEARS

Left: A pink Chiltern bear from the 1930s (left) and a 1920s Papa Moritz bear with a musical bellows movement.

HOORAY FOR BEARS!

These jolly little Teddy Bears,

Who always love to play,

When hugged by little boys and girls,

They'll scare all gloom away

Anonymous

Left: a splendid early Steiff bear from 1908.

On his 100th birthday, the old-fashioned teddy bear remains a highly desirable object. In the 20th century he became a major icon and childhood classic.

For arctophiles, as bear-lovers are sometimes known, the market for old bears and teddy bear ephemera has become firmly established. The bear artists who make high-quality hand-crafted bears in the traditional manner have long waiting lists. Bear fairs, teddy bear stores and direct mail enable collectors with even the slimmest purses to pursue their hobby.

For all bear lovers there is now a wealth of information available on care, repair and restoration, display and storage. No-one who is interested in and loves teddy bears can complain that they are left out.

In the 21st century knowledge and information are easily accessed worldwide. For all bear lovers this assures the future of the treasure trove of teddies which we have inherited. From the little crippled German girl who made her family's name famously synonymous with the classic cuddly teddy bear, to the American president who refused to shoot a tethered animal – chance established the teddy bear fever which has remained a part of our heritage.

From famous star bears to anonymous beloved threadbare friends – worldwide, the future of the teddy bear could not be brighter.

HOORAY FOR BEARS!

Perhaps the wonderful world of replica bears – which offers collectors the chance to recreate teddy bear history and a nostalgic retreat to the past – is the way into the 21st century. And what of the future?

Many of the long-established manufacturers fortunately archived their early design information. Some of these designs have been recreated and now collectors are able to enjoy classic teddy bears a second time round.

But what exactly are replica bears? Because many collectors are now trying to achieve a complete set of a manufacturer's original range, and bears from before the First and Second World War are more and more elusive, replicas are the nearest they can get to the original.

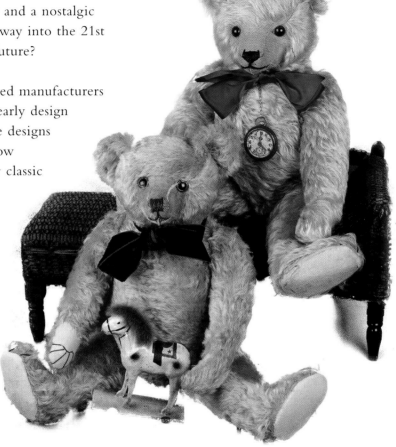

Left: Original Farnell bears.

Below: Two 1908 Seiff bears sit back to back.

A replica bear is one which has been faithfully recreated – a facsimile of some of the original manufacturer's designs. The price range of bears like the early Steiffs is well beyond the pocket of most ordinary people these days and replicas are the nearest thing to the original early bears which were, when they were first launched, simply intended as gifts for children.

Today, however, teddy bears are increasingly seen as collector's items to be enjoyed by adults who often regard them as heirlooms of the future. Of course, replica bears may not appeal to everyone and it is a matter of personal taste. There are many collectors of modest means who would much prefer to own an original old Steiff teddy bear even if it has the scars to prove that it was literally loved to bits. Others would rather have a bear which is in pristine condition, with documentation backing up its provenance and a limited edition number to be passed on should they ever decide to sell.

There is no doubt that a replica bear will accurately reflect the original design which appeared years ago, and if these bears are collected they do make a lovely display when they are all in identical condition.

It was in 1984 that the enthusiasm for replica bears reached its peak. All the major manufacturers were reproducing old designs or creating special new ones. A UK survey at the time showed that an amazing 40 per cent of all teddy bears being sold were bought for adults not children.

Steiff, which had always prided itself on its image as a maker of children's toys, was forced to review its position. The wave of nostalgia which was impossible to ignore prompted Steiff to publish a facsimile of its 1892 catalogue together with a postcard booklet of early bears. This was followed by a series of replicas and wherever possible these were made to the same pattern, using similar materials as the originals.

It was not always possible for Steiff to achieve exact copies. The famous Teddy Rose of 1925 was made without its original soft, light kapok stuffing which was replaced with excelsior, and the 1927 favourite Bulldog Billy reappeared without his ruff in 1986.

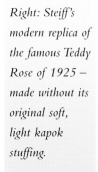

Right: Steiff's modern replica of the famous Teddy Rose of 1925 – made without its original soft, light kapok stuffing.

HOORAY FOR BEARS!

All the original Steiff bears on which the replicas are based are either displayed in the Steiff museum in Giengen or listed in their archives. For example, in 1980 when Steiff celebrated its 100th anniversary, a replica of the 1930 Original Teddy was issued as a limited edition of 5,000 for the US and 6,000 for Germany. It was made to the old pattern in high-quality mohair, stuffed with excelsior and with lovely glass eyes. At that time, teddy nostalgia had not yet hit Germany and initially the bear just did not sell in its home country. Today, this Original Teddy is one of the most highly prized and valuable of the Steiff replica bears.

Of course, the success of the Steiff replicas grew as the years went on and an annual programme was put in place, adding more and more bears each year. At first some were made in quite large numbers. This was a mistake because collectors thought that these bears were too common and so were reluctant to buy them. Throughout the 1980s it was normal for production runs to number 10,000 replica teddy bears. By 1995 the company began reducing editions to a maximum of 5,000 and today some of the replicas appear in very small limited numbers. Some collectors find it impossible to obtain the bears they want.

Left: Steiff's replica Teddy Clown.

HOORAY FOR BEARS!

The 1926 Clown is one of the most popular Steiff replicas available today. It is made of lovely rose pink mohair and has felt paws, with brown and black eyes, a brown nose and claws. It wears a clown hat and a ruff and is stuffed with wood shavings. This is one of the most nostalgic designs. Produced in 1999, the Clown bear is limited to 5,000 and is clearly in great demand once more.

To stimulate interest among collectors, some Steiff replicas are made in restricted numbers, for sale exclusively in the US or only available for a short time. This makes them highly desirable and very much sought after amongst replica collectors.

Right: An original 1920s Steiff Clown bear.

In 1984, other major manufacturers followed Steiff's lead. History was repeating itself. America's Ideal Novelty

and Toy Company decided to introduce porcelain replicas of its very first 1903 bear. The German Gebrüder Hermann started to expand its business to include adult collectibles although it still produced toys for children. In 1984, it brought out Model 63 – a replica of the first Gebrüder Hermann bear. And, of course, very quickly other special editions and replica bears followed. Bernhard Bear, who was named after the company's original owner, appeared. Then it was the turn of the Sonneberg Bear, a 1991 replica of the 1922 design which was produced in a limited edition of 4,000. The identifying card carried by this bear reflects Sonneberg's long history of making wooden toys, with its picture of a toy horse.

Left: 'Bears of the Round Table' by Sigikid.

Bernhard's company had at first operated from what was to become East Germany, until the family were forced to flee to Coburg in the west where they built up their business again. They still keep their proud history alive with regular appearances of replica teddy bears.

Another very old German company with a history dating back to the mid-19th century, called Sigikid, entered the market in 1992,

producing replica soft toys based on old patterns which had been discovered in Czechoslovakia. After the Communist takeover of Hamiro, once the second-largest toy manufacturer in Europe, the patterns had been squirrelled away in an attic. Descendants of the former owner of the factory, Karel Pospisil, recreated the old animals. Production was set up again near to the original factory in Bohemia and the Miro collection of replicas was added to the Sigikid catalogue.

HOORAY FOR BEARS!

In 1986, British companies began to expand into the adult collectors' market. Merrythought brought out a replica of their Magnet bear, a 1930s chunky teddy with sturdy limbs and large ears. In 1990 a lavender-tipped version appeared. In the 1930s the original had been part of a series of floral-scented bears which had included Peach Blossom, Petal and Rose. Merrythought also produced various replicas of celebrity teddy bears.

In 1992, two famous facsimiles appeared: from Bing, Gatti a 6-inch bear which had survived the sinking of the *Titanic* with his owner, Luigi Gatti; and from Merrythought, Mr Whoppit, which had accompanied Donald Campbell, the holder of the land and water speed record, on his journeys. This bear from the Cheeky range actually survived his owner's last journey which ended fatally on Lake Windermere.

Right:
Merrythought's
Cheeky bear.

HOORAY FOR BEARS!

Throughout the 1990s Dean's made available their range of Collectors Club replicas which recreated the traditional features of their early British bears, using designs from their archives.

So, the story of the teddy bear has come full circle. The opportunity to collect the wonderful replicas now being made is recreating teddy bear history with very special nostalgic additions to this timeless childhood classic.

What to Do Next

As a teddy bear lover, you might want to take your hobby further now that you have read the story of how the teddy bear became so famous.

Wherever you live in the world there will be something for you, and I am including an annual calendar of events, useful names and addresses, teddy bear manufacturers, magazines devoted to teddy bears and a list of teddy bear artists. There should be something for everyone who loves and celebrates the teddy bear.

Left: An unusual pair of Farnell bears in a rare colour dating back to 1920 (left) and 1930 (right).

HOORAY FOR BEARS!

Right: These cheeky looking bears are Russian and sport the Olympic logo. They were produced as souvenirs for the Olympic games held in Moscow.

HOORAY FOR BEARS!

GLOSSARY

ANNIVERSARY BEAR

A bear made by a well known or long-established teddy bear manufacturer which is intended to mark an important date.

ARTIFICIAL SILK PLUSH (OR ART SILK PLUSH)

A man-made fibre which was produced from cotton or wood and was used for teddy bears from about 1930.

ARTIST BEAR

A teddy bear which is designed and made by one person who sometimes uses others to help. It is finished by hand.

BAT-WING NOSE

A distinctive type of stitching which resembles bat wings.

BOOT-BUTTON EYES

These are black wooden eyes which have metal loops on the back. They are similar in appearance to old-fashioned boot buttons and were particularly popular for the earliest teddy bear eyes.

BURLAP (ALSO KNOWN AS HESSIAN)

A heavy coarse fabric which is woven from hemp or jute and used for some early stuffed toys.

CELLULOID

A man-made material produced from a type of cellulose and camphor, called pyroxylin.

CLIPPED MOHAIR

A mohair which has been cut short and is used on the muzzle or the tops of the feet.

COTTON PLUSH

A cheap material which is woven from cotton. It was used on bears at the time of the Second World War.

GLOSSARY

COTTON WASTE/SUB

The waste which was left over from the manufacture of cotton in factories. It was introduced as stuffing for British bears after the First World War because other materials were hard to obtain.

DISTRESSED MOHAIR

A mohair plush which is made to look antique. It is popular among manufacturers producing replicas and bear artists.

DUAL PLUSH
(ALSO KNOWN AS TIPPED MOHAIR)

A mohair which has had the ends painted with a second colour.

EXCELSIOR/WOOD WOOL

A soft mixture of long thin wood shavings which is used for stuffing.

FOOT PADS

The bottom of the feet, usually made of felt, rexine or leather.

GOOGLY EYES

These eyes are distinctively round and large, often moveable and glance to the side.

GROWLER

The voice box which produces a roar or growl.

HUMP

The pronounced lump on the back of a bear which was introduced by Steiff. It was copied by other manufacturers in the early 20th century.

INSET MUZZLE

A muzzle made of a separate piece of material which is sewn into the face.

JOINTED BEARS

These have moveable arms, legs and heads.

KAPOK

A lightweight silky fibre which is derived from a seed pod and used for stuffing.

LATEX

A natural material which is used to produce rubber.

LIMITED EDITION TEDDY BEARS

These are produced in a limited number which makes them especially collectible.

GLOSSARY

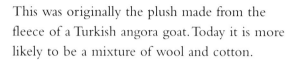

MOHAIR PLUSH

This was originally the plush made from the fleece of a Turkish angora goat. Today it is more likely to be a mixture of wool and cotton.

PAW PADS

The pads at the end of a bear's arms.

PLUSH

A fabric which has a cut pile which is softer and longer than velvet.

REPLICA

A direct copy of an antique teddy bear. It is produced in limited numbers by the original manufacturer and often uses old factory patterns.

REXINE

A shiny oilskin or leather cloth material which was used for paw pads. It was popular for English bears after the Second World War. Often the coating has worn off over time which leaves a cotton backing.

ROD BEAR

A type of bear which was introduced by Steiff. It has metal rodded joints running through the body.

SEALING WAX

A wax which was produced to seal documents and used during the early 20th century to make realistic moulded noses for teddy bears.

STICK BEAR

A small cheaply made bear, usually unjointed, made in the US in huge quantities.

SUB (SEE COTTON WASTE)

SWING TAG

A paper identification tag which is printed with the manufacturer's details and attached to a bear.

TIPPED (SEE DUAL PLUSH)

ULTRASUEDE

A synthetic suede-like material which was used for paw pads. First introduced in the US.

WEBBED CLAW STITCHING

This was used particularly by Merrythought and Farnell to produce distinctive claws.

YES/NO

A type of teddy bear which was produced by Schuco, the German manufacturer. By moving the tail, the head can be turned up and down or from left to right.

ZOTTY BEAR

A long-haired teddy bear introduced by Steiff which has an open mouth. It was later copied by other manufacturers.

ANNUAL CALENDAR OF EVENTS

TEDDY BEAR, DOLL AND ANTIQUE TOY SHOW AND SALE

Linda Mullins – San Diego, California, US.

DOLLS, BEARS, SUPPLIES AND COLLECTIBLES SHOW AND SALE

San Diego,California, US.

TEDDY BEAR SHOW AND SALE

ABC Unlimited, Arizona, US.

BEARS ONLY

Stratford Civic Hall, Stratford upon Avon, England.

CONVENTION AND ALL TEDDY BEAR SHOW AND SALE

Seattle, Washington, US.

POLICHINELLE (FRENCH DOLLS FAIR)

Usually held in Paris, France.

THE WINTER BEAR FEST

Kensington Town Hall, Hornton Street, London W8, England.

WINTER TEDDY BEAR EXTRAVAGANZA

Newport ,Rhode Island, US.

DOLL, TOY, BEAR SHOW

Lansing, Michigan, US

JAPAN TEDDY BEAR FESTIVAL

Tokyo, Japan

TEDDY BEAR EXTRAVAGANZA

Northboro, Maine, US

APRIL

ANNUAL DOLL AND BEAR SHOW AND SALE

Jamesburg, New Jersey, US.

ANNUAL CALENDAR OF EVENTS

DOLLS, BEARS, SUPPLIES AND COLLECTIBLES SHOW SALE

San Diego, California, US.

EASTERN STATES DOLL, TOY AND TEDDY BEAR SHOW

West Springfield, Massachusetts, US.

THE LONDON BEAR FAIR

Fairfield Halls, Croydon, Surrey, England.

MIDLAND TEDDY BEAR FESTIVAL

Telford Moat House, Telford, England.

TEDDY BEAR CONVENTION AUCTION, SHOW AND SALE

Schaumburg, Illinois, US

TOY MANIA

Parc des Expositions, Porte de Versailles, Paris 15e, France.

THE BEAR SHOW AND SALE

San Mateo, California, US.

DOLL AND TEDDY BEAR SHOW AND SALE

Portland, Oregon, USA.

THE FESTIVAL OF ARTIST BEARS

Civic Hall, Stratford upon Avon, England.

ANNUAL BEAR SHOW AND SALE

Tampa, Florida, US.

TEDDY BEAR FESTIVAL AND SHOW AND SALE

Rochester, New York, US.

TEDDY BEAR JUBILEE

Overland Park, Kansas, US

WINTER WONDERLAND

Brisbane City Hall, Brisbane, Queensland, Australia.

ANNUAL TEDDY BEAR SHOW AND SALE

San Jose, California, US.

AUSTRALIA'S PREMIER BEAR AFFAIR

Sydney Town Hall, Sydney, Australia.

ANNUAL CALENDAR OF EVENTS

FESTIVAL OF STEIFF

The Toy Store, Toledo, Ohio, US.

BRITISH TEDDY BEAR FESTIVAL

Kensington Town Hall, Hornton Street,
London W8, England.

ROCKY MOUNTAIN TEDDIES

Copper Mountain, Colorado, US.

SOUTH AUSTRALIAN DOLL AND TEDDY SHOW

Adelaide Festival Centre, Adelaide, Australia.

TEDDY BEAR SHOW AND CONVENTION

Timonium, Maryland, US.

THE TEDDY BEAR CLUB FAIR

Hobart Town Hall, Hobart, Tasmania,
Australia.

PREMIER DOLL AND TEDDY BEAR SHOW

Huntington, New York, US.

DOLL AND TEDDY BEAR COLLECTORS SHOW

Sydney Town Hall, Sydney, Australia.

DREAM CATCHERS DOLLS AND BEARS SHOW AND SALE

Phoenix, Arizona, US.

JAPAN TEDDY BEAR FESTIVAL

Kobe, Japan.

POLICHINELLE DOLLS FAIR

Paris, France.

BEARS ON PARADE AT THE FAIR

Flemington Racecourse, Flemington,
Victoria, Australia,

TEDDY BEAR SHOW AND SALE

Atlanta, Georgia, US.

THE BRITISH BEAR FAIR

Hove Town Hall, Horton Road, Hove,
Nr Brighton, England.

TOY MANIA

Parc des Expositions, Port de Versailles, Paris,
France.

*Left: A 1930s
Chiltern bear.*

USEFUL ADDRESSES

Clubs and Associations

ENGLAND

THE BRITISH BEAR CLUB

Avalon Court, Star Road, Partridge Green,

West Sussex RH13 8RY

Telephone: 01403 711511

BRITISH TEDDY BEAR ASSOCIATION

PO Box 290, Brighton,

East Sussex BN2 1DR

Telephone: 01273 697974

IRELAND

BEAR FRIENDS

Mount Windsor, Farnahoe,

Inishannon, Co. Cork.

Telephone: 353 21 775470

JAPAN

JAPAN TEDDY BEAR FAN CLUB

2-3 Nangu-Cho Ashiya-City,

Hyogo 659.

Telephone: 81 797 23 5533

JAPAN TEDDY BEAR ASSOCIATION

Komatsu-bldg,

16-20 Nanpeidai-cho,

Shibuya-ku, Tokyo 150.

UNITED STATES

GOOD BEARS OF THE WORLD

PO Box 13907, Toledo,

OH 43613

STEIFF CLUB USA

225 Fifth Avenue, Suite 1033,

New York, NY 10010

USEFUL ADDRESSES

Teddy Bear Magazines

AUSTRALIA

BEAR FACTS REVIEW

PO Box 503, Moss Vale,
NSW 2577
Telephone: 61 48 6781 338

ENGLAND

HUGGLETS TEDDY BEAR MAGAZINE/ HUGGLETS UK TEDDY BEAR GUIDE

PO Box 290, Brighton BN2 1DR
Telephone: 01273 697974

TEDDY BEAR TIMES

Avalon Court, Star Road,
Partridge Green, West Sussex RH13 8R.
Telephone: 01403 711511

FRANCE

CLUB FRANCAIS DE L'OURS ANCIEN

Boite 7082,
70, rue Lieu de Sante,
76000 Rouen
Telephone: 33 35 88 9600

JAPAN

TEDDY BEAR POST

Japan Teddy Bear Fan Club,
2–3 Nangu-Cho, Ashiya City,
Hyogo 659.

UNITED STATES OF AMERICA

TEDDY BEAR AND FRIENDS

Cowles Magazines Inc.,
6405 Flank Drive,
Harrisburg, PA 17112

THE TEDDY BEAR REVIEW

PO Box 1239, Hanover,
PA 17331

THE TEDDY BEAR TIMES

State Line Road,
North Bend, Cincinnati,
OH 45052

USEFUL ADDRESSES

Teddy Bear Museums

UNITED KINGDOM

THE LONDON TOY AND MODEL MUSEUM

21–23 Craven Hill, London W2 3EN

THE TEDDY BEAR MUSEUM

19 Greenhill Street, Stratford upon Avon,
Warwickshire CV37 6LF

TEDDY MELROSE

The High Street, Melrose,
Roxburghshire TED6 9PA, Scotland.

GERMANY

MARGARETE STEIFF MUSEUM

Giengen an der Brenz.

SWITZERLAND

SPIELZEUGMUSEUM

Baselstrasse 34,
CH-4125 Richen

UNITED STATES OF AMERICA

TEDDY BEAR MUSEUM OF NAPLES

2511 Pine Ridge Road,
Naples, FL 33942

INDEX

INDEX

INDEX

INDEX

INDEX

W